*New York City
and the Fair*

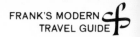

NEW YORK CITY

Unisphere ® presented by (USS) United States Steel

© 1961 New York World's Fair 1964-1965 Corporation

and the
FAIR
1964-1965

by Lucrecia López

Photographs by
Thomas Henion

CHARLES FRANK PUBLICATIONS, INC.

432 Park Avenue South, New York, N. Y.

Library of Congress Catalog Card Number: 64-22539

Photographs by Thomas Henion
Copyright 1964 by TREMONT ASSOCIATES, INC.

Printed in the United States of America

Table
of Contents

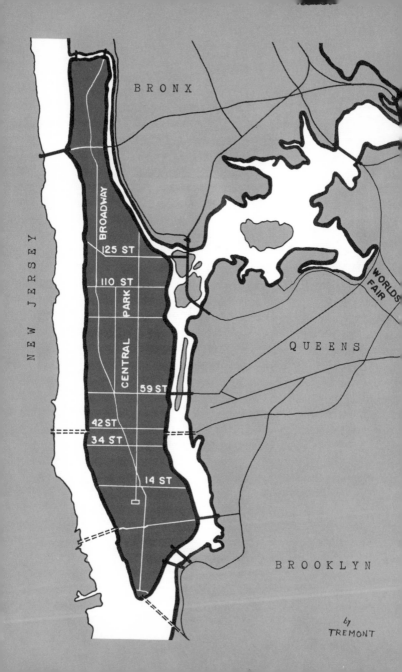

Introduction

The literal-minded can give you a long list of what New York City *is*. They'll tell you, for example, that it is a city of some 8 million people —all squeezed into 320 square miles (the more precise will put it at 319.8 square miles). They'll point out that supersaturated Manhattan has a population density of 75,072 per square mile —greatly augmented by 14 million visitors annually. They might also mention that it is a city of five boroughs — Queens, Brooklyn, Richmond, the Bronx and Manhattan, in descending order of size— and that it has more than 800,000 buildings (one for every ten New Yorkers) and over 100 bridges connecting the boroughs to each other, and to the United States. Here they may point out that New York City also happens to be an island city with approximately 86% of its area swimming in the Atlantic Ocean separated from the mainland.

When it comes to New York City's population, the literal minded also have another long list. New York City is the largest "Indian village" in the United States —3,362 American Indians live in it. It's also the largest Puerto Rican city —its Puerto Rican population is half again as large as that of San Juan, Puerto Rico's capital and largest city. It's the second largest Irish city —only Dublin,

Ireland's capital, has a larger Irish population. New York City is even large for Italian and Russian cities —it has almost one million Italians and more than half a million Russians. In short, about 50% of New York City's population is in fact either foreign born or born of foreign parents. (This percentage does not include the Puerto Ricans who are Americans.)

New York is also a city of transients —mostly young hopefuls who arrive with stars in their eyes, intent on conquering the world— a wonderful breed until they become bitter because they don't have what it takes to make the grade. Be leery, consequently, of the persons who talk about the "typical" New Yorker. Either they just don't know what they're talking about —or they're stretching the truth to score a point. To use that old and famous expression, there ain't no such animal.

Neither the literal-minded nor the poetically inclined —nor New Yorkers, themselves— can paint New York the way it really is: one of the most fascinating and exciting cities in the world, one that has to be seen to be believed.

1

300 Years in the Making

The New Yorker (let's define him as someone who has been living in New York for the past decade and has no immediate intentions of leaving) thinks of his great city—if he stops to think of it at all—as a bustling, modern metropolis where the one sure thing is *change*: a city in transit from an obliterated past to a rather uncertain future.

No one would be more surprised to learn than he that his children —at least, some New Yorker's children— may be swinging on the gate that once swung open to the hand of George Washington and Alexander Hamilton. New York, in fact, for all its steel and glass skyscrapers, is quite hoary as American cities go. It has seen an awful lot of American history in the making—more than 3½ centuries of it. It has made an awful lot of American history, itself —the New York Historical Society has a whole library to prove it.

Recorded history for New York began back in 1524. In that year one Giovanni da Verrazano, an Italian explorer-priate —pirateering was a favorite and respectable sport for any sailor worth his salt and bullion-laden Spanish galleons were the game— in the pay of France passed through the strait between Staten Island and Brooklyn, today known as the "Narrows," and entered New York Harbor. Giovanni liked what he saw — "a very agreeable spot located within two small prominent hills in the midst of which flowed to the sea a very great river, deep within the mouth." (How right he was. New York harbor is considered one of the most perfect natural harbors in the world because of its sheltered position, access and ample water area and depth.) Navigator Verrazano didn't do much after that: he named the great bay "Santa Margarita" for reasons of his own and the great river and surrounding countryside Angouême in honor of the man who was paying his bread and butter —Francis I, of the royal family of Angouême. Then he sailed away. Neither name stuck but a statue stands in Battery Park to remind Anglo-Saxon New Yorkers that an intrepid Italian was there long before the Dutch or the British and the longest suspension span in the world connecting Staten Island with Brooklyn bears the name of the Verrazano-Narrows Bridge for historically accurate reasons.

Then, around the late 1500's, European nations began outbidding each other for the services of venturesome sailors willing to risk their skins for a few pieces of silver to find a shorter passage to China and India via the northern part of Russia. In 1596 the Netherlands even went so far as to offer a prize of $10,000 to anyone discovering the short cut to the fabulous East. By 1608 an English mariner by the name of Henry Hudson succeeded in going further north than anyone had ever been before. The Dutch, panicked by the certainty that Hudson was on the right track —or rather, sea lane— and that they were about to lose the sea race to the British, sent

Verrazano-Narrows Bridge under construction

post-haste for the British mariner. Those early Dutch were good life insurance salesmen. Hudson worked out a deal with them whereby he would receive $320 for his services in a sea hunt for the northeast passage; his wife, $80 should he not return.

On April 4th, 1609 Hudson and a motley crew set sail from Texel, Holland in the 80-ton "Half Moon." On September 2nd, 1609, the Half Moon finally anchored off Sandy Hook and on the succeeding three weeks

Hudson & Co. explored the great harbor and river nearby. When the English navigator returned to Holland, the pelts of beaver, otter, marten and fox he had had the foresight to bring back with him did much to mollify the piqued directors of the Dutch East India Company who had their hearts set on a northeast passage.

For a time, not much else happened of note. True, in 1611, Adriaen Bloch, a Dutch merchant hove into view bent on doing business with the numerous Indians Henry Hudson had reported seeing shuttling back and forth across the bay. Bloch accomplished his mission and, presumably, was the first to enter Long Island Sound. Then, in 1615, the New Netherlands Company acquired exclusive trading rights with the Indians in this part of the New World for three years. They built a fort, a storehouse and a few huts on the lower tip of Manhattan.

Historical Barter

It was only in 1624, a century after Verrazano first sighted that "pleasant" spot, that Manhattan felt its first "big" wave of immigration —30 protestant Walloon families arrived, of which eight men stayed on Manhattan and the remainder went to settle in Fort Orange (now Albany). During the next two years the early settlement went through two directors and a minor population explosion. When the first director general —irascible Peter Minuit— arrived on the scene in 1626, the population had climbed to 200. This was the year that Minuit —or the Indians, some claim— perpetrated the biggest swindle on record: for $24 worth of clothes, trinkets and beads the Indians were persuaded to turn over the Island of Manhattan to the Dutch. The most amazing part of the entire transaction was that it ever occurred at all: in other parts of the New World, the newcomers took what they saw without bothering to consult —or recompense— the inhabitants. Nonetheless, despite his amicable settlement with the natives, Minuit took the sensible precaution of erecting a fort —Fort Amsterdam— and then he made the settlement, Nieuw Amsterdam, the capital.

Today the Dutch population of New York City is so small as to be scarcely noticeable. (After all, why leave crowded Holland for crowded Manhattan?) Nevertheless, though much of what they left behind has been or is fast being reduced to rubble under the hydraulic hammers of a wrecking crew, the early Dutch did much to shape the destiny of the City.

Unlike their puritanical neighbors to the north, these first New Yorkers were a boisterous, tolerant bunch. They accepted in their midst the Quakers, Jews and other sects and peoples that the less tolerant Puritans would not admit. New York became then as it is now the melting pot of the New World. By the time the English took over in 1664, 18 languages were spoken on Manhattan. By that time, too, the other communities springing up along the coast were beginning to look down their noses in horror at the roistering mynheers and to call Manhattan the Devil's capital (a title the city "regained" two centuries or so later). One third of the Dutch houses —or so the scandalized (or was it envious?) neighbors claimed— were taverns and they all seemed to be doing a thriving business.

In the meantime, management of the Dutch settlement went from bad to impossible. The directors appointed by the Dutch West India Company to look after its interests in the New World were, on the whole, an unsavory lot. They cared little for the public and —far from the parent company's eye— the company's welfare. Many took advantage of their dictatorial position to enrich their own bins —and thus started a trend which, alas, was to continue throughout New York City's history. For example, during his five year tenure (1633-1638) as fifth director general of Nieuw Amsterdam, Wouter Van Twiller (and friends) managed to acquire about 15,000 acres of Long Island land through personal negotiations with the Indians. Van Twiller was eventually recalled because of his mismanagement —but not before he had acquired (in addition to his Long Island holdings) a farm to the north of the settlement (and thus became the founder of Greenwich Village) and Nutten Island just off the tip of southern Manhattan (today known as Governor's Island for that reason).

The next governor, Willem Kieft, tried to be better. He passed countless edicts designed to reform Cain-raising citizens of Nieuw Amsterdam —unsuccessfully. Then he committed the imbecility of having more than 80 Indians (including women and children) slaughtered in in their sleep in reprisal for the murder of one reprehensible Claes Smits who some years before had killed an Indian for his beaver skins. The enraged Indians —eleven tribes of them— determined to exterminate the intruders and for two years systematically set about accomplishing their purpose. They very nearly succeeded. By the end of the two years only 100 live and terror-stricken settlers remained and most of them wanted the head of Willem Kieft.

The Indians eventually sued for peace —they had to tend to their spring planting— but the amicable spirit present during the Manhattan Island transaction was gone forever. And Wall Street, where "a good solid fence" was built as protection against the hostile Indians came into being, if not in name at least in spirit. (In 1652 Peter Stuyvesant had a real thick wall built not so much as protection from hostile Indians as from the hostile British soldiers he was expecting from the north. The "wall" is still there —an almost solid wall of skyscrapers occupied by New York's financial giants.)

Kieft was finally recalled but before his ship reached Holland it struck a rock and he was saved the embarrassment of having to face the irate directors of the Dutch West Indian Company who were much concerned because their lucrative investment in the New World was threatened. Replacement for Kieft came in the shape of wooden-legged, iron-fisted Peter Stuyvesant who listed anti-Semitism among his questionable virtues. (His 17th century wig would have curled had he realized his Nieuw Amsterdam was to become the metropolis with the largest Jewish population in the world.)

Stiff-necked dictator Stuyvesant ruled with a will and a heart of steel and as such was probably the best administrator the city had ever had. In 1658 he established the first "rattle watch" of Nieuw Amsterdam's "finest" —eight men who might be considered New York City's first police force. Nonetheless, try as he might, issue edicts and ordinances as he did, nothing seemed to curb the over-exuberance of his rowdy citizens. At one point Governor Stuyvesant raised the fine for striking another from $2.40 to $10 because the fighting Dutch deemed the former fine a cheap enough price to pay for the satisfaction of venting their spleen on each other.

When the British took over Nieuw Amsterdam in 1664, despite the change in name (the now English settlement was named in honor of the Duke of York) and in government, the local citizenry remained much the same —an independent, fighting lot. For a while the British contented themselves with just the change in name but, gradually, they attempted to place greater and greater controls on the city government —and gradually New York's ever-expanding population insisted on self-determination.

To many New Yorkers, Boston was the beginning and the end of the American Revolution. Few realize the role their city played in paving the road to American Independence. By 1683 the Dutch (and English) merchants of New York were refusing to pay the duties levied on them under the "Duke's Laws." By the mid-1700's New York City was not only considered the center of trade of the colonies but the center of resistance to royal rule —a fact which lead to its early downfall for the British decided the revolution would be short lived if the center of resistance were first taken.

Birth of 'St. Tammany'

By the mid 1700's, too, groups loyal to George III had organized into the societies of St. George, St. Andrew, St. David, etc. As a countermove the rebellious faction organized the Sons of Liberty, known too as the Sons of St. Tammany. The Tammany was after Tammanend, a wise and liberty-loving Delaware Indian Chief; the St. was thrown in gratuitously as a tongue-in-check mimicking of the royalist societies.

The Society of St. Tammany was revived after the Revolution by a New York upholsterer, William Moody, and represented middle class opposition to the aristocratic and property class who in the 1780's had succeeded in limiting suffrage to freeholders. The Society of St. Tammany, in fact, was instrumental in the election of Thomas Jefferson. Historians today, however, prefer to refer to the revolutionists as the Sons of Liberty ever since the days in the mid-1800's when a corrupt Tammany (by then the ruling force in New York City's politics) lost its halo and never quite managed to regain it.

When the British parliament was so rash as to pass the Stamp Act, New York City's newspaper denounced the measure. A Stamp Act Congress was held in New York's City Hall which was attended by representatives of all the colonies. The arrival of the British ship in New York Harbor with the stamps further incited New York's already incited citizens. A group of the Sons of Liberty hung Governor Cadwallader Colden in effigy almost literally under his very nose. The citizens continued their staunch resistance to the Stamp Act and the British Parliament finally —temporarily— became practical and repealed it. While New Yorkers were patting each other on the back, the Sons of Liberty erected a "liberty pole" in the town commons —now City Hall Park. It became one of their favorite pastimes much to the exasperation of the British who had the trouble of cutting them down.

The Patriotic Brew

When Lord North sent a tea-laden ship to New York with the intent of carrying out his taxation policies, New Yorkers —headed by a committee of the Sons of Liberty— had their own tea party: they tossed overboard a few chests of tea, sent the ship packing back to England —and took to drinking that patriotic brew, coffee. When the British in retaliation for the Boston Tea Party closed the port of Boston, New Yorkers promptly responded by calling a meeting —held at New York City's historic Fraunces Tavern— and elected a committee of 51. The Committee of 51, in turn, issued the call for the first congress of the colonies. Subsequently, when news of the Battle of Lexington reached New York, angry mobs seized City Hall and the munitions stored there. The day

George Washington arrived in New York on his way to Boston, though the colony was still —at least in theory— loyal to King George, cheering New Yorkers lined up along Broadway and welcomed him with what was probably the city's first ticker tape parade.

With the evacuation of Boston, Washington moved his headquarters to New York. On July 12th, 1776, Adm. Richard Howe arrived on the scene with a royal fleet, but he waited anchored in New York Harbor for more than a month before landing his troops. In the face of superior forces, Washington's position was untenable and he was slowly forced to retreat first from Long Island (a monument on a hill in the Brooklyn Heights section commemorates the battle) and then to the upper part of Manhattan. There, in the Battle of Harlem Heights (approximately opposite the west front of Columbia University) the revolutionists forced the British to retreat —temporarily. A week after the Battle of Harlem Heights, New York had its first great fire destroying the lower part of the city almost completely. On the same day a young school teacher was captured out on Long Island, accused of spying and shortly after was tried by a British military court, condemned and hanged. Manhattan's skyscrapers today look down on the spot at 46th Street and First Avenue where Nathan Hale defiantly regretted he had but one life to give for his country.

A month or so later, Howe pushed northward again until ultimately Washington was forced to abandon Manhattan. From that moment until Cornwallis' capitulation at Yorktown, New Yorkers chafed under British military occupation. New York City became a vast prison camp. Out on the East River, an old hulk used by the British as a war prison became a death ship for 11,000 prisoners of war. In lower Manhattan the buildings razed by the

fire were replaced by huts and tents used mostly by out-
laws and thieves. Lawlessness, disease and economic re-
strictions well nigh wrecked the once thriving port.

On October 19th, 1781, Cornwallis surrendered,
virtually ending the Revolution though preliminary articles of peace were not signed until November of 1782
and a definitive peace treaty was not concluded until
September 3, 1783. On November 25th, 1783 New York
was finally evacuated by the British and on December 4th,
1783 George Washington chose Fraunces Tavern to bid
a sad (and famous) farewell to his officers. With the
British evacuation and the return of unrestricted trade,
business slowly revived. Nonetheless, by 1787 New York
City's almhouse sheltered 300 destitutes. Bankruptcies
were so prevalent and debtors' prisons so filled that at
one point New York City assemblymen contributed a
part of their salaries to relieve the debtors in prison.

Yet New York City's recuperative powers were
sufficient for her to be made the first capital of the infant
nation. On April 30th, 1789 Washington took his inaugural oath on the steps of Federal Hall at the now
famous meeting of Broad and Wall Streets. Though a
little more than a year later the capital was changed to
Philadelphia pending the building of Washington, D.C.,
New York City kept growing and drawing people and
business to it. It became the center of events that were to
shape the destiny of the nation.

John Fitch in 1796 tried out his steamboat models
on Collect Pond (now the land filled in beyond City Hall)
and portended the doom of the beautiful clipper ships.
On July 11th, 1804 Aaron Burr, in a duel, killed Alexander Hamilton and robbed the city of one of its favorite
sons and a nation of a first rate mind. Hamilton was
buried in a crypt in Trinity Church and Burr, unable to

tolerate the odium of New Yorkers, fled to the south. There, while he dreamt of building empires, New York City under Mayor De Witt Clinton grew rapidly and prospered. (Aaron Burr eventually returned to New York City and years later, for a brief period, enjoyed some of that prosperity —he married Madame Jumel, said to be the richest woman in the country, the widow of a French merchant who had brought his wealth to Manhattan.)

Then the Embargo Act of 1807, forbidding foreign commerce altogether, hit the prosperous port of New York in the solar plexus. With the War of 1812 New Yorkers were even worse off. Washington D.C. was burnt by the British and once again New York City became a center for troops. About this time the city's fortifications were built and strengthened in preparation for a British attack that never materialized. What the British failed to do, all-conquering time accomplished: except for the eight-foot thick walls of Castle Clinton at Battery Park and a blockhouse in Central Park, little remains of NewYork's old line of defense. Today, instead, Nike bases baring slender missiles to the sky defend New York City —and the American people.

At the end of the War of 1812 New York again demonstrated its remarkable recuperative powers. The clipper ships that had helped defeat the British now helped it regain its position as America's prosperous, leading port. Great waves of immigrants attracted by the hope of a better life pounded on its harbor doors and were admitted. New Yorkers saw the start of their first housing problem —a problem that has been with them in varying degrees of severity ever since. The city's sanitation and other public facilities were taxed beyond the limit. Yellow fever epidemics broke out killing thousands and New York's wealthy in panic deserted the disease-ridden city for the pure air of the "countryside." Greenwich Village, incubating since the time that Governor Wouter Van Twiller had purchased his farm, was hatched and became the center of High Society.

The specter of disease, however, was not enough to frighten off prosperity. By 1824 New York City had become the nation's leading manufacturing city, a position it has held ever since. In 1835 another great fire broke out destroying almost all of the city below Wall Street. But neither disease nor fire could prevent New York's fantastic growth. By this time New Yorkers numbered over 200,000 and the residential center had moved as far north as Union Square —so-called because it was the point at which the city's two main avenues, Bowery Road and Broadway, met.

The Road to Culture

By 1850 New York City was the publishing and cultural center of the United States. "Cultured" New Yorkers, recently become music-conscious, flocked to Castle Gardens (the former Fort Clinton) to see and hear P. T. Barnum's amazing new European import —Jenny Lind, the Swedish Nightingale. Three years later New York City felt itself big enough to imitate flourishing London and New Yorkers had their first (and the world's second) world's fair —a smashing success but a financial failure. But New York was a city of millionaires by then and could well afford such financial setbacks. Progress and society, all undaunted, continued what seemed to be their manifest destiny towards the Harlem River. In 1856, Central Park was purchased by the City to preserve at least 840 acres of Manhattan Island from being gobbled up by both.

This, too, was the era in which an uneasy madness

gripped the city and the nation over the issues of slavery and state's rights. Whispers of secession were, in some cases, changing to shouts. In 1861 even the mayor —more dishonest than most and with a weathervane for a head— suggested that New York City secede from the Union and become a city-state collecting its own custom duties, etc. (The possibilities for additional graft were enormous.) The suggestion, fortunately, fell on deaf ears though, at first, many New Yorkers sympathized with the southern cause and President-elect Lincoln was hanged in effigy from the mast of ships docked in the harbor.

A Rich Man's War

With the firing on and surrender of Fort Sumter, New Yorkers, almost to a man, lined themselves up behind Lincoln and the millionaire city authorized a million dollar loan to save the Union. Once again New York was filled with soldiers. The policy of conscription, however, which permitted draft deferment through the payment of $300, gave rise to the people's claim that the Civil War was "a rich man's war and a poor man's fight." New York's ugly and disastrous draft riots resulted —some claim they were politically instigated— and it took the police five days to control. By that time hundreds had been killed and more than 50 buildings destroyed. Civil War and draft riots notwithstanding, New York continued its northward march.

In 1866, the Black Crook, New York City's first "Broadway production," began its long and successful career. It subsequently took to the road and Broadway became a common household word throughout the United States. In 1870 another long and successful career was started —that of the Brooklyn Bridge, an engineering marvel for those days. The 70's, too, saw the birth of the

The Brooklyn Bridge and a view of the Manhattan skyline

infamous Tammany Tweed Ring which with aplomb and an almost completely free hand swindled New York City taxpayers out of some $200 million. Left from this period of corruption is the City Court Building which depleted the city treasury of $12 million —about six times the true construction costs.

The Naughty Nineties found the city not much

better off as far as corruption was concerned but vice was making the headlines. East side, west side, all around the town, brothels flourished under the nose of (and, in fact, with the blessing of) the police —provided, of course, appropriate libations were made to them in the form of a percentage of the house's take or a stipulated premium for "insurance" or an occasional "donation" for a policeman in need. The elite section of Brothel Row —in mid-Manhattan along Sixth Avenue and its side streets— was very elite indeed. In one of these establishments, during certain nights of the year, evening clothes were expected —at least, to be admitted. Another, an establishment which took in several street numbers —and differing tastes— had the brotherly title of "The House of All Nations" and the furnishings to match.

From these bawdy years, New York City inherited the brownstone houses, first the fashionable homes of High Society (and of the "better" brothels), then during Prohibition days, the address of the speakeasies. Most of these brownstones have crumbled into slums or have given way to the numerous housing projects that have sprung up all around Manhattan.

Along with graft, vice, the Brooklyn Bridge and the brownstones, the late 1800's also brought to New York City an ever-extending city limits: in 1874 the city jumped the Harlem River to take in some of the Bronx within its corporate arms and for the first time, New York City was joined to the mainland of the United States; in 1895 the city pushed itself as far as Yonkers and Mount Vernon; in 1898 it swam the East River and the Upper Bay to swallow Brooklyn, Staten Island and part of Queens and thus was born Greater New York.

With the extension of the city limits, New Yorkers needed more than ever a rapid means of transporation to get them from their homes to their jobs. (A steam-drawn Ninth Avenue El had been put into operation back in 1870 and other "Els" had followed but they could scarcely be considered "rapid.") Then in 1900 New Yorkers were given a hint of the coming bane (and salvation) of their daily existence. Plans for the first subway were announced. Four years later it was in operation. Today the city's subway system carries almost 1½ billion passengers annually over 236.7 route miles of running track.

The early 1900's saw the start of the skyscraper boom. An achitectural it-can't-be-done —the Flatiron Building— went up first in 1902. The Metropolitan Life Insurance Building (50 stories) and the Chanin Building (56 stories) followed shortly after. In 1913 up went the Woolworth Building which held the corner on the tall buildings market until the Chrysler (1930) and the Empire State Buildings (1931) captured the title. (The latter, as E. B. White put it, managed to reach the highest point in the sky at the lowest moment of the depression.)

The 'Dry' Era

The Roaring Twenties and Prohibition found New Yorkers very thirsty indeed. Speakeasies sprang up like crabgrass in suburbia —usually decorously ensconced in the old brownstone town houses of the fashionable. According to one story, a die-hard dowager who had clung to her brownstone in the West Fifties, was bothered so often by thirsty New Yorkers and visitors in a search of a speakeasy that she had a sign placed on her door: *"This is NOT an illicit resort."* New York City's famous El Morocco, the Stork Club and the exclusive 21 Club are all direct descendants of speakeasies from these dry times.

Despite the depression —or more probably, because of it (and WPA workers and funds)— the late 20's and 30's saw a frenzy of construction. By 1927 car-owning New Yorkers had one more link with their New Jersey neighbors —the Holland tunnel connecting lower Manhattan with Jersey City. By 1931 New Yorkers could cross the Hudson to New Jersey's Fort Lee via the beautiful George Washington Bridge with a suspension span twice as along as any previously constructed. In 1931, too, as the finishing touches were being put on the Empire State Building, work was begun on Rockefeller Plaza.

The 1920's, too, saw a rise in crime and corruption in political office —both familiar situations to blasé New Yorkers. With the depression, however, they were in no mood for such shenanigans. In 1932, New York City's playboy mayor, Jimmy Walker (better known to New Yorkers for his popularity than for his honesty) was summoned before then Governor Franklin D. Roosevelt to answer charges of graft brought against his administration. He chose to resign instead. It was a turning point in the city's administration. In 1933 New York's beloved, comic-reading, squeaky-voiced Fiorello H. LaGuardia was elected mayor and for 12 years (he was re-elected twice) New Yorkers were aware that honest, efficient government was possible.

Under LaGuardia's administration New York City's highways were extended and new ones were built. In 1936 the fabulous Triborough Bridge and its highways were open to the public and in 1937 New Yorkers were again joined up with Jerseyites via the Lincoln Tunnel connecting midtown Manhattan with Weehawken. The year 1939 brought three important events: eastern Bronx was united with Queens by one of New York's most beautiful bridges, the Bronx-Whitestone Bridge; LaGuardia Airport, one of the world's busiest, opened in time to welcome the flocks of visitors flying in to see the third important and by far most popular event of the year —New York City's "World of Tomorrow," the 1939-1940 World's Fair— held on re-claimed Flushing Meadow swamps, later to become Flushing Meadow Park, also the site of the 1964-1965 World's Fair.

The 1940's saw New Yorkers faced with a war and wartime rationing. The city's "brown-out" turned the Gay White Way into a pallid ghost of its former self. For once Manhattan's traffic problem was solved —gasoline rationing forcibly reduced the number of cars on the road. Construction slowed down to a snail's pace —but only temporarily— while attention was turned to the instruments of war. Many New Yorkers daily left their city to work in the defense plants out on Long Island.

Then, by the late 40's and early 50's, New York City was bursting its seams again. It appeared to have reached about as far —and as high— as it could go. To escape the crowds and the congestion, New Yorkers again began desserting their city for the wilds of the suburbs —Long Island and Westchester— but they returned for eight hours every day to earn their bread and butter. New parkways were built and old ones widened to handle the increased commutation from the suburbs but these became obsolete before the work on them was completed. The late 50's and early 60's witnessed (are witnessing) another frenzy of construction. A new bumper crop of skyscrapers changed the New York skyline into an almost solid wall of glass, steel and reinforced concrete. The Lever Brothers Building started the trend with a glass and steel cantilever design daring for those days. The trend, to date, shows no signs of stopping. Fifth, Park and Third Avenues have become glittering showcases of the International Style in architecture. Third

Avenue, in particular, has been given such a face-lifting that even its best friends can hardly recognize it. First step in the plastic surgery was the tearing down of the ancient Third Avenue El and the tearing up of the even ancienter cobblestone street. Then, tall, steel and glass office buildings replaced the dirty, crumbling tenements. At night long slender fluorescent lamps leaning over the broad avenue bathe it in a white light. Today, more dignified and quiet than the gaudy Broadway and Times Square area, Third Avenue, more than any other street in New York City deserves the title of "The Great White Way."

But the construction bug hasn't infected only the east side of Manhattan. You'll find the executioner's mark on old (and sometimes new) buildings throughout the city: a huge white "X" on the windows indicating that room has been vacated and is ready to go. Even the disreputable Bowery is beginning to take on fine airs. Few tears will be shed over most of the horrors slated for the wrecking crew. Perhaps some of the old, picturesque streets of Greenwich Village should be spared but here too the dreaded white X has been seen. The truth is that some parts of the Village could (and probably will) stand a face-lifting, too.

This guide, in fact, is being written in the full and frustrating knowledge that with each peck of the typewriter, the experts at demolishing and constructing are, somewhere, changing the face of New York and that in hundreds of offices throughout this fantastic city, other experts at the drafting board are designing changes that will make this guide "old" by tomorrow. There's no help for it. If you want to see New York City the way it is *now,* don't bother packing. Just take the first jet out —you may make it.

2

A Few
Essential Facts

The advice of your friends and relatives to the contrary notwithstanding, you've decided to spend your vacation in New York City. Congratulations. Now that your mind is made up the rest is easy. All roads lead to New York. So do all major airlines, railroad lines, steamship lines, bus lines. Some people have come by bicycle; others, walking. One notorious case arrived on a raft. All you have to do is decide which means is best suited to your pocketbook, the time at your disposal, your physical capacity and your personal inclinations.

What will you need?

If you're American, all you need to come to New York City is the wherewithal. This may mean anything from $10.00 a day (plus transportation) to you-name-it —depending upon how high you may want to live on the hog. You may even make it on less than $10.00 per day if: 1) you're lucky enough to find a room at the William Sloane House of the YMCA or, 2) if you have no objection to sleeping in a Bowery flophouse and, 3) if you're willing to cut corners on such things as breakfast, lunch and dinner. Many of New York City's top sights are, believe it or not, free. In any case, there are plenty of free ones to keep you busy during your stay so that you can save your pennies for the essentials. Of course, you may not be able to lunch at the *21 Club* or dine and dance at *El Morocco,* but you will be able to enjoy a complete dinner at Chinatown ($1.30) and an excellent production of Shakespeare in the Park (free).

If you're not American, to enter the United States you'll need the wherewithal —and some documents as well. Ask at the American consulate nearest you for the necessary forms. Health and immigration requirements differ depending upon the country of origin but chances are that as a tourist you will only need an easily obtained visitor's visa and a valid small pox vaccination certificate.

What should you pack?

That will all depend upon the time of year you decide to take New York by storm. Some people prefer New York City in springtime when the Japanese Cherry blossoms have made a pink heaven out of the Brooklyn Botanical Gardens —light topcoat-raincoat weather. Others like summertime when New York puts on its festival and you may hear and see Shakespeare's plays and music in the city's parks and sleep on white sandy beaches. Bathing suits and short-sleeved cotton shirts and dresses are the order of the day. Still others like autumn when there's a nip in the air and the trees are putting on their annual fashion show (topcoat and sweater weather), while Christmas in New York can be cold but it is almost always beautiful. (This is bundling up weather —don't forget your storm boots.)

Incidentally, not even New Yorkers will believe this, but it's true: New York City averages more hours of sunshine than Nice —Nice of the bikinis on the French Riviera. Nevertheless, whether you come when it's subzero weather or 93° F. in the shade of a skyscraper, the ladies had best pack a sweater. It will come in handy for New York City's air-conditioned restaurants and theaters. The men may want to pack at least one jacket and tie —some restaurants will not admit them without either.

Don't forget to pack this guide!

Where will you stay?

New York City has more than 700 hotels, motels and tourist courts from which to choose. The majority of Manhattan's hotels are in the midtown section —naturally— in the center of things. The cost of a room may vary anywhere from the 35c a night charged by a Bowery flophouse to $90 a night for the most luxurious suite.

A comprehensive selection of hotels —covering the gamut of prices— is listed alphabetically in the appendix on page 247. Since what a father of five may consider exorbitant, a gay blade on an expense account may consider inexpensive, no attempt has been made to classify these hotels into the usual guidebook categories of inexpensive, moderate, expensive, etc. Furthermore, the price of the least expensive room in a so-called luxury hotel often overlaps with some of the prices charged by the "moderate" hotels so that such categories become meaningless. Consequently, the list of hotels in the appendix merely gives the address, telephone number and price ranges for single and double rooms with bath —and no editorial comment. After studying the list you will be able to supply your own —probably ranging from "hmm??" to "wow"! depending upon the girth of your wallet.

The "fashionable" hotels at this writing are the

new Hotel Americana and the New York Hilton at Rockefeller Center. Equally (if not more) fashionable without
as much publicity are the Carlyle, (where the late President and Jackie Kennedy stayed), the Regency, the
Pierre, the Plaza, the Essex House, the Hampshire House
Hotels (all overlooking Central Park). Then, of course,
there is always the Waldorf Astoria, probably New York's
best known hotel, where for as little as $10 a night you
can say you slept with royalty.

Don't let the comparatively low rates of some of the
hotels on the list worry you. All the hotels listed provide
comfortable if not always plush accommodations —you
needn't be ashamed of stopping with your family at anyone of them.

Some sound advice: New York is a city in flux.
Make your hotel reservations in advance and be sure to
check the rates at the time: telephone numbers and rates
may change without advanced warning.

Where will you eat?

If you enjoy eating, you'll find that dining in New
York will be one of your greatest adventures and pleasures. This hungry city has over 10,000 places where you
may eat anything from a snack to a Polynesian luau,
depending upon your wallet and your gastric capacity;
where —gustatorily speaking— you may go from Argentina to Zanzibar without traveling more than 15 miles.

In the appendix on page 253 you will find an alphabetical list of more than 75 New York restaurants giving
the address, telephone number, type of restaurant (i.e.,
French, Italian, etc.), some of the specialties and the
minimum prices offered. The list is by no means complete
nor does it include all the different nationalities in New
York City's restaurant world. It does, however, include

some of the finest restaurants in the United States, ranking with the best in Paris, and it offers a more than ample selection for all types of budgets, all types of tastes. In addition, on the theory that one's apt to develop an appetite while sightseeing, at the beginning of each chapter, you will find a list of restaurants in the part of New York being covered. You can check these restaurants for address, specialties, prices, etc. in the alphabetical listing.

The restaurants presently making the greatest "splash" in New York City are the Restaurant Associates trio: "The Forum of the Twelve Caesars," the "Four Seasons" and "La Fonda del Sol." These three combine lavish and exotic decors with good, often exotic food —and high to very high prices. You'll find few restaurants in town as interesting to the eye as these three but many equally (or, often, more) pleasing to the palate —and at lower prices. La Fonda del Sol, for example, specializes in Latin American cooking but most Latin Americans (who should know) prefer the less showy, less well known, *less expensive* Liborio for their favorite dishes. Nonetheless, the striking and colorful setting of La Fonda del Sol is alone worth the price while those not accustomed to eating this type of food back home will find it delicious.

A few other, traditional restaurants, without the decor, match (and often may surpass) the prices of the Restaurant Associates trio —but the food is superb. Le Pavillon, for example, ranks as one of the world's great restaurants —which is undoubtedly why the prices are so high and you must make reservations in advance.

Don't, however, turn up your nose at the smaller, more modest establishments. You'll find that many on the list —usually specializing in foreign cuisine— fall in this category and they are by and large excellent. Don't, for that matter, neglect the Horn and Hardart automats scattered throughout New York City. The food is good, the selection large, the pies about the most delicious anywhere and the prices among the most reasonable in town. For the best buy on a steak, baked potato, tossed salad, bread, butter and coffee, try Tad's Steaks: $1.29 will buy the meal but outside of a limited selection of deserts, you have no other choice. If you'll settle for a hamburger, etc., try any one of the various Prexy's scattered around the city where the hamburgers served "have a college education" —and are good besides. You'll like their "soft ice cream," too —a form of frozen custard. The Chock Full o' Nuts chain is also fine if all you want is a sandwich or a coffee break. Their donuts (especially the whole wheat ones) are delicious.

For delicious cold meat sandwiches, don't overlook the delicatessens —especially those in foreign neighborhoods. In the days before Third Avenue became refined, on a pleasant day you could find no better lunch in town than a 45c baked ham and cheese sandwich (about an inch thick) on old fashioned Swedish rye bought at a Swedish delicatessen in the shadow of the El. A short stroll east brought you to the East River and a park bench where you could sit and munch while you watched the tugs chug by and idly wondered how many sparrows make a summer. The El and the Swedish delicatessen are gone but there are other similar delicatessens east side, west side and the tugs on the East River continue to chug by.

Wining and Dining after Hours

Besides the Statue of Liberty and the Empire State Building, there is very little else as basic on visitors' "must do" lists as to take in some of New York City's notorious night life. They won't be disappointed in two

Nyeela, a prime attraction at the Round Table

things: in its length —Manhattan never seems to sleep though by 3 a.m. the tempo has slowed down— and in its variety. They'll find the big, plushy nightclubs relying heavily on the undraped shape of their chorus line to draw attention and the cozy, intimate *boîtes* with soft lights, a small dance floor and a select floor show. There are the smoke-filled dens where the revues are satirical or where jazz is the order of the day but where the dance floor. is non-existent. On the other hand, there are the large dance halls where the dance floor is enormous, the two alternating orchestras excellent and the dancers themselves the best and only floor show. Then there are the clubs for the deviationists where girls dance with girls or where, if you go unbriefed, you'll be thoroughly surprised to discover that the stripteaser with the smooth, peaches and cream skin is male. (The term is used loosely.)

The Appendix on page 263 lists some of New York City's better known nightclubs. Take your pick. Incidentally, though all nightclubs serve food —of sorts— it is generally over-priced and under par. Your best bet is to dine at a good restaurant and save your drinking for the nightclub. Some clubs have a cover charge. Others, however, have a minimum charge that isn't too minimum. Some people find this a challenge and slowly proceed to get drunk attempting to consume the minimum. They would have been better off eating at the nightclub.

Of Rest and Restrooms

In Paris a man caught far from home or his hotel room rarely has a problem: he'll find quite obvious public latrines located at strategic corners along the way. In Manhattan things are a little different. New Yorkers have the same basic necessities but the approach is much more coy. Though on the surface it looks as though Manhattan hasn't any toilet facilities, actually they are liberally scattered throughout the island. It's just a question of knowing where to look for them. If you suddenly find yourself in need, don't panic. Knock on any of the following doors:

If it's a ladies' room you need, walk or run to the nearest department store or women's specialty shop. They know which side their bread is buttered on and cater to all feminine needs and desires. Airline, busline and railroad terminals have public facilities for both sexes; so do most hotels near their restaurant or cocktail lounge or off the lobby. Museums and other tourist attractions have facilities. Then there's the nearest bar —but they'll feel more kindly if you order a beer before using their lavatory— or the nearest restaurant, but first order a snack. As a last resort, try the public lavoratories of the subways. Every station has one for both men and women but they are usually malodorous and dirty.

If, on the other hand, what you're seeking is relief for your aching feet, the following will provide a chance for rest and relaxation: waiting rooms of the airline, bus-line and railroad terminals; lobbies of major hotels; the nearest library; the park benches along the East and Hudson Rivers, in all the city parks and along the Promenade Gardens at Rockefeller Center.

How to Get Around New York City

Getting around Manhattan, where most of New York City's principal attractions lie, is relatively easy. Manhattan is small —a mere 22.6 square miles; 13.4 miles long and 2.3 miles at its greatest width— the smallest of the five boroughs. If you get lost in it, it won't be irretrievably. The same isn't true of the remaining 297 square miles of the city. If you plan to visit the outlying boroughs, be sure you receive complete and explicit instructions from your concierge not only on how to get there but, more important, on how to get back.

To simplify matters, Manhattan (above Greenwich Village) is laid out like a grid with the streets and avenues numbered progressively —except for wayward Broadway and a few after thoughts. The streets run across the entire width of the island starting from 13th Street and proceeding in an orderly numerical sequence as far north as 193rd Street. The Avenues, running lengthwise across the island start with First Avenue and end with Twelfth with a few extra strays cut in. The avenues, in short, have the following sequence: First Avenue; Second Avenue; Third Avenue; Lexington Avenue —cut in above 23rd Street; Fourth (or Park) Avenue; Madison Avenue —cut in above 23rd Street; Fifth Avenue —the dividing line between the east and west, between the haves and havenots; Avenue of the Americas, officially, though New Yorkers persist on calling it Sixth Avenue —called Lenox Avenue above 110th Street; Seventh Avenue; Eighth Avenue —called Central Park West above 59th Street; Ninth Avenue —called Columbus Avenue above 59th Street; Tenth Avenue —called Amsterdam Avenue above 59th Street; Eleventh Avenue —called West End Avenue above 59th Street; Twelfth Avenue —ending at 72nd Street.

In this fairly orderly scheme of things, the chief clown is erratic Broadway. At the level of Washington Square (in Greenwich Village), Broadway is east of Fifth Avenue. It suddenly slants west so that by 23rd Street it is west of Fifth and by 72nd, west of Tenth.

Midtown Manhattan, consequently, is reasonably easy to navigate, but lower Manhattan (below 13th Street) and, to a lesser extent, the upper tip of Manhattan (above 193rd Street) are covered by a helter-skelter network of short streets and require frequent consultation with a map to explore. Of course, you may wander about aimlessly with no fixed goal in mind, but maps are provided herein in case you prefer the former method.

With a map of New York indelibly engraved on your brain, the next problem is *how do you get about?*

■ By car

If you've thought of driving in Manhattan, promptly put the thought right out of your mind. Only mad dogs and taxi cab drivers venture out in Manhattan traffic. Anyone else so rash as to attempt it almost invariably winds up on the fringe of a nervous breakdown and with a dented fender. Furthermore, you will find that Manhattan traffic snarls are such that practically any other form of transportation —including walking— is quicker than by car. Lastly, finding a parking space in Manhattan (unless it's uptown or in an expensive parking lot) is next to impossible. Consequently, if you drove from out of town to New York City, park your car in a nice, safe garage and use any of the following:

▪ **Your own two feet**

The only real way to see most of Manhattan is by walking. You should plan to cover a feasible area each day on foot, taking a subway or other means of transportation to your starting and from your finishing point. Future chapters of this guide cover Manhattan section by section and explain the quickest and easiest way to arrive at your first stop —and your walking route thereafter.

▪ **By Subway**

By far the cheapest and often the quickest and most efficient way to get around town is via New York City's rapid transit system consisting of three separate subway lines which cover the city almost entirely with a network of tracks. The cost of a ride on any one of these lines is 15c and you may make your ride as short or as long as you want it. However, to change from one subway line to another you generally must pay an additional 15c token unless you make the transfer at certain designated points.

A young New Yorker from Flushing, by doubling back where necessary, managed to ride over the transit system's 237 miles of running track on one 15c token. He chalked up 400 miles on the trip —a distance greater than from New York to Pittsburgh— a fantastic transportation buy.

The three lines operated by the Transit Authority are the BMT (Brooklyn-Manhattan Transit), the IND (Independent) and the IRT (Interborough Rapid Transit) each having several branches and each branch covering a different route and operating both express and local trains along that route. Express trains stop only at express stations but the local trains stop at all stations.

The quickest way by subway to any point is to take the express train to the express stop nearest your destination and from that point take the local train to the proper stop. That's the quickest way. Very often, when the trains are crowded, the most comfortable way is to take the local train —where you are more liable to find a seat and breathing space— all the way. Lastly, if ever this book has any sound advice to offer, the soundest is this: if you value your life and limb, don't ride the subways during rush hours. All the stories you have heard about subway riders being packed into cars like sardines in a can are perfectly true —except, perhaps, that the sardines have more elbow room. To be on the safe side, avoid subways between 7 and 9:30 a.m. and 4:30 and 6 p.m.

The BMT operates mostly in Brooklyn though it services Manhattan below Central Park primarily along Broadway. The IND operates in the Bronx, Brooklyn, Manhattan and Queens. In Manhattan, the IND covers Sixth and Eighth Avenues going as far as Washington Heights in the northernmost trip of the island.

The IRT also covers the Bronx, Brooklyn, Manhattan and Queens, but it covers Manhattan and the Bronx best. In Manhattan, the IRT-Lexington Avenue covers Lexington Avenue for its entire length, while the IRT-Broadway-Seventh Avenue line first runs along Seventh Avenue and then, above 50th Street, along Broadway until 96th Street. Here the Seventh Avenue line branches off and continues along Lenox Avenue while the Broadway line continues along Broadway to the Bronx.

However, before you promptly proceed to lose

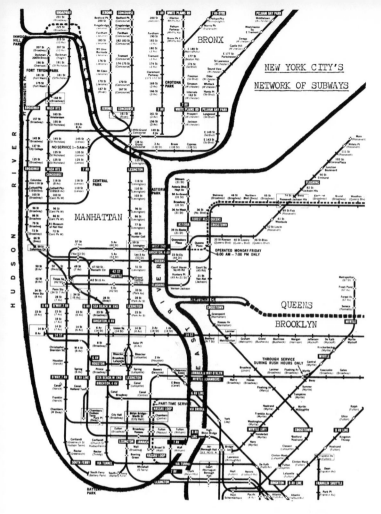

yourself on New York City's subways, ask the gentlemen at any of the booths selling tokens for the free Official New York Subway Map and Guide. The map clearly shows all the express and local stops in the entire subway system as well as the routes followed by the three main subway lines. Once armed with this you'll find that getting about New York is really quite easy —underground.

■ By Bus

New York City has buses galore, usually belching black noxious fumes and hogging the road —and charging 15c for their stop-and-go ride along Manhattan's congested streets. These buses cover (or leave you within short walking distance) of practically every corner in Manhattan, but they have unsettling ways of deviating unexpectedly from an avenue or a street. (A good deal of this seemingly erratic behavior has to do with one-way streets and the like.)

The Manhattan-Bronx Surface Transit Operating Authority (more chummily called MaBSTOA), which is the mastermind behind this transportation system, recently printed a 72 page booklet just noting the essential details of its different routes. Obviously, what MaBSTOA does so concisely in 72 pages cannot be reduced here to a paragraph. Suffice it to say that buses run all day long along Manhattan's avenues and on the following crosstown streets: Spring-Delancey Streets, Houston Street-Avenue C, 8th, 14th, 23rd, 34th, 42nd, 57th, 72nd, 79th, 86th, 96th, 108th, 116th and 125th Streets.

There are bus stops generally at the corners of every other block and all are clearly marked. You'll also find maps at these stops indicating the bus route. However, before you drop your 15c in the coin box, be sure to ask the driver if his bus is going where you want it to go. If it's not, he'll tell you which one is.

Buses are not meant to be taken by those in a hurry —not only because the buses have to fight traffic most of the way, but because they must make stops almost every two blocks. However, for a combined leisurely ride and economical tour of Manhattan, take the No. 4 bus marked Fort Tyron Park-Pennsylvania Station. You may pick it up along West 32nd Street or along

Fifth Avenue above 32nd Street. From Fifth Avenue the bus turns west on 110th Street and goes down Cathedral Parkway and then up pleasant Riverside Drive and Fort Washington Avenue to beautiful Fort Tyron Park.

■ By Taxi

Taxicabs are a traffic hazard, but they can be an answer to your prayer if you're in a great rush —but not to get across town— or if you're longing for restful privacy and comfort. Comparatively speaking, they're not too expensive either: they charge the lowest metered rates in the country. New York City's taxicab drivers have the *sang-froid* —and complete disregard for pedestrians and other cars— needed to drive successfully in Manhattan. Consequently, they're usually the quickest distance between two points along the avenues. If, however, you must go any distance crosstown anywhere in midtown Manhattan, you'll be able to make it faster walking because even the most skillful and cold-blooded cab drivers are powerless against crosstown traffic.

■ By boat

You may also literally get around Manhattan by boat: the Circle Line (CI 6-3200, JU 6-5300) at Pier 81 at the foot of West 41st have 3-hour, 35-mile long cruises around Manhattan Island leaving four times daily. The price for the cruise —one of the most pleasant and restful ways visitors have of seeing Manhattan— is $2.75 for adults, $1.25 for children.

Now that you know how to get about Manhattan, take four to get ready —and let's go.

Give me your tired,
your poor;
your huddled masses
yearning to breathe
free; the wretched
refuse of your
teeming shores...

Emma Lazarus

Section	From Battery Park to City Hall.
Map	See page 46.
First stop	IRT-Lexington Avenue (express stop) or IRT-Broadway (local stop) to South Ferry (Battery Park); BMT (via tunnel) to Whitehall (South Ferry) — local stop.
Where to eat	Fraunces Tavern, Kabuki, Miller's, Oscar's Delmonico, Sieburg's Buffet, Whyte's. (Refer to appendix for details.) Also snack bars at the Statue of Liberty and Staten Island Ferry and the cafeteria at the Seamen's Church Institute.
Sights for the children	Castle Clinton, Statue of Liberty, Staten Island Ferryboat ride, Marine Museum of the Seamen's Church Institute, Fraunces Tavern, Federal Hall, Trefflich Bird and and Animal Company.

3

The Solid
Gold Front

If you want to be logical about it —though few people use logic either in coming to New York, talking about New York or seeing New York. (It's usually rose-colored or spleen-colored glasses.)— If you want to be logical about it, the most logical place to start your tour of New York City is at the southern tip of Manhattan where the city began as a handful of huts and a fort and, from such small beginnings, metastasized into the monstrous metropolis of today with its more than 800,000 buildings —most of which (at least, so it appears) are either in the process of going up or being torn down.

Battery Park

New York's first handful of huts and a fort were erected in that part of southern Manhattan known as Battery Park and for a long while it remained the island's most densely populated area. Today the Battery is about

by
TREMONT

the only clearing in a forest of skyscrapers. Lower Manhattan takes first prize for having the greatest concentration of tall buildings —and the lowest concentration of permanent residents. The population ebbs and flows with the waves of commuting office dwellers that (weekdays) break and recede on its shores —and weekends disappear altogether.

This is the section of New York City where many dreams begin —and, alas, many dreams fade; where ocean liners bring the world's poor —and its rich, too— for their first glimpse of America; where the city's greatest wealth is accumulated —not too far from the Bowery where the city's worst destitutes are (more than likely) intoxicated. It is also the section of the city where you can have your cheapest or your wildest fling —a five-cent ferry ride or shooting the works on the stock market. It's as good a place as any to become acquainted with New York.

■ New York Harbor

Start with a walk along the promenade edging the harbor and take a good look out on the rippling waters. It's not very pretty —practically any other harbor in the world is prettier— but it happens to be the greatest, most naturally protected, busiest harbor in the world and it has made New York City the incredible, fascinating, soul-devouring monster that it is. (Most New Yorkers have forgotten —if they ever knew— that their wonderful town is, above all, a seaport.)

If you like to watch ships coming in and out of the harbor, New York is the place for it. Sit on one of the Park's benches and just wait. New York Harbor has an average of 70 such comings and goings in a day. Usually the ocean liners sail past your right to the North pier docks while the less romantic but more rugged cargo ships chug past your left headed for the East River docks.

If you don't have all day to sit around, take a look at the shipping news section of the *New York Times*. It lists arrivals and departures and you can time your own arrival at Battery Park accordingly.

(Incidentally, those who have a yearning to board one of the giants of the ocean may now satisfy it: a 50c contribution to the Seamen's Welfare Fund will get you a pass to board any of the liners docked on the Hudson River piers up to a half hour before departure time. Passes are usually available at a booth next to the entrance ramp of whichever ship you decide to visit.)

Out in the harbor on your right you can make out Ellis Island, that part of the United States which millions of immigrants first knew as "home." The tidal waves of immigrants that pounded New York's shores during the 19th and first half of the 20th century have dwindled down to a mere drip and New York and New Jersey are vying with each other to see who will first convert Ellis Island into a recreational center —but all this is still in the let's see stage.

To the left is Governor's Island, first the property of Gov. Wouter Van Twiller (1634), now the home of the First Army. Historic Castle Williams —one of New York City's early defenses— serves as a military prison. The only visitors to the island are those who have special passes obtained from Army headquarters. If you're one of the lucky ones, the pass entitles you to a free ride on a government-operated ferry leaving from a terminal on the eastern end of Battery Park.

The most familiar, most thrilling sight, though is directly in front: Liberty Island with its principal and famous resident, the Statue of Liberty, holding her head and her torch high and looking down her classic nose at the ships, tugs, barges, what-have-you that push past her

S.S. United States gets a scrubdown at its pier in New York Harbor

The Marine Memorial for the East Coast, dedicated to the men and women who died in Atlantic Coastal Waters during the Second World War

hems. She's worth a closer look, that grand old lady, but for the moment turn your attention to Battery Park, itself. It probably has about the greatest collection of monuments —some of them horrors— ever accumulated within 22.985 acres (the size of the Park).

■ The Monuments

You may start by first depositing your brood —the smaller ones who don't appreciate statuary, if you've brought them in tow— in the small, fenced-in playground on the east corner of the Park. Directly south of the playground stands the *Coast Guard Memorial,* a bronze group dedicated to the men and women of the Coast Guard who lost their lives during the Second World War.

To the right of it, beautifully austere and impressive, is New York City's most recently erected monument

—the *Marine Memorial for the East Coast,* two rows of
eight tall, stark granite slabs each with row upon grim row
of names of the men and women, "Members of All Armed
Services of the Second World War Who Sleep in American Coastal Waters of the Atlantic Ocean." Between the
granite slabs, looking out to sea and to the Statue of Liberty, as though it had just alighted on a crag, perches an
almost-in-motion bronze sculpture of the American Eagle.
Its pedestal of polished, black granite bears the simple
dedication quoted above.

Over-shadowed —almost lost— by the Marine
Memorial and to its left stands the Wireless Operator's
Memorial, a small simple fountain dedicated to those wire-
less operators who lost their lives at sea while on duty.
Next to it, virtually radiating vitality, stands the striking
bronze figure of that intrepid Florentine, *Giovanni da Ver-*

razano who, though naught came of it, discovered New York for the French in 1524. The statue was donated by a large group of Italian-American citizens who like to remind New Yorkers of who discovered their harbor first.

Castle Clinton

Next to the statue of Verrazano, sitting round and squat, is Castle Clinton which took part in a good deal of New York City's history before it settled down to being a staid national monument. Castle Clinton started life as a straightforward harbor fortification, the last in a series of forts erected to guard lower Manhattan (in this case, from the British during the Napoleonic Era) and the direct descendant of a waterside battery which had protected New York Ctiy as far back as 1689.

The fort, built some 200 feet off the southwest end of Manhattan, was called West Battery and was connected to Manhattan by a timber drawbridge causeway. Completed in the fall of 1811 —just in time for the War of 1812— the fort fired its guns for the first time on "Evacuation Day" (November 25th) in a memorial salute to the British evacuation of New York City at the end of the American Revolution. It was the first and one of the few times. Except for target practice and some 21-gun salutes, the fort has never fired a shot. The British threat to New York City never materialized —possibly because of its defenses— and the fort (by then renamed Castle Clinton after the city's dynamic Mayor DeWitt Clinton) was eventually ceded to the city.

New York City's authorities, recognizing the Castle's potential, decided to make an honest dollar by leasing it as a place of entertainment. The Castle was remodeled and landscaped accordingly. In July 1824 it opened as "Castle Garden" and soon became a favorite spot for dances, concerts —and any important city event. Samuel B. Morse, in fact, demonstrated the telegraph there in 1842, and on September 11th, 1850, Jenny Lind scored the musical triumph of the century singing to (and winning the hearts of) a record-breaking, normally tone-deaf American audience.

The rumor is that it wasn't so much the voice of the Swedish Nightingale —lovely though it was— that packed Castle Garden that night as it was the remarkable show-manship of that incredible fellow, Phineas Taylor Barnum. In any case, Jenny Lind's first performance was the start of New York's questionable but thriving ticket specula-tion business. One ticket was sold for $225 to a Man-hattan hatter who afterwards became known as the "Mad Hatter." There was method in his madness, however. The resulting publicity was worth ten times the amount he had paid for the ticket.

Nothing —not even Jenny Lind— could top that first performance and eventually Castle Garden was leased to the New York State Commissioner of Emigration and opened as an Emigration Landing Depot. By that time, the 200 feet of water separating it from Manhattan were filled in and the Castle became part of the "mainland." For the next 35 years Castle Garden served as the gate for the 7 million immigrants —Irish, Germans, Poles, Russians, Italians, etc.— who came pouring in. But finally even Castle Clinton couldn't hold the vast hordes that knocked at New York City's doors, and the immigrants were moved to newer quarters —Ellis Island. Thereafter the fort was once more altered to accommodate perhaps its most famous tenant —the fabulous New York City Aquarium (now moved to Coney Island). On its open-ing day in 1896, 30,000 people came to gape at the Aquarium's piscatorial wonders.

When the plans for the Brooklyn-Battery Tunnel (passing underneath the Battery) were being translated from paper into action, Castle Clinton was slated for the executioner's block (or the wrecking crew's hammer). A group of nostalgic —but influential— New Yorkers prevented its destruction: an Act of Congress established it as a national monument.

If you continue to circle Battery Park, you'll also come upon: 1.) The Walloon Monument dedicated to New York's first Dutch settlers; 2) the statue of John Ericsson, designer of the "Monitor," first turreted battle-ship; 3) a plaque to the Salvation Army; etc., before you turn full circle back to the playground and your offspring.

Statue of Liberty

Just south of the playground is a building where you may buy round trip tickets for the Statue of Liberty ferry —and have a snack while you wait for departure time. The fare to Liberty Island —80c for adults, 40c for children under 12— is one of the best sightseeing buys New York City has to offer. Ferries leave every hour on the hour (on the half hour, too, in summer), give you a wonderful opportunity to take photographs of Lower Manhattan's receding forest of skyscrapers, a pleasant 20-minute sea voyage trip, some more wonderful opportunities to take shots of the approaching giant statue and, finally, the chance to practically shake hands with America's most famous symbol and monument.

The statue's symbolism is obvious: at her feet lie the broken chains of tyranny; in one hand she holds a tablet inscribed with that famous date —July 4th, 1776; in the other hand, the torch held high is a beacon lighting the way to liberty. At night it casts a glow —the National Park Service assures us— equivalent to 2500 full moons.

The words to Emma Lazarus' famous sonnet are engraved on a tablet inside the statue's 150-foot high pedestal. But Liberty is remarkable in a great number of other ways not the least of which is that she was a gift of the *people* of France —not the government— to the people of the United States. The entire cost of the colossal statue —about $250,000— was raised by popular subscription. The American people, on the other hand, donated the $225,000 needed to erect the pedestal.

Its construction is another remarkable point. The sculptor, an Alsatian by the name of Frederic Auguste Bartholdi, had to enlarge his 9-foot working model almost 17 times to attain the statue's height of 152 feet. The work had to be done section by section. The lady is made up of copper sheets, about the thickness of a half a dollar, hammered by hand into shape and later assembled. (Her light green color, in fact, is due to the oxidation of these copper sheets.) You'll get some idea of her tremendous size if you just visualize her eyes —each measures 2½ feet across. Few people realize that this giantess' framework was designed by the French engineer famous for his tower —Gustave Eiffel. The framework had to be good —it has to withstand the high winds of the lower Bay.

When the Statue of Liberty was first opened to the public, visitors —if they were sound of wind and limb— could make the climb up to a narrow balcony surrounding the torch. That part of the excursion became too dangerous and it had to be closed. Today you may take an elevator ride (for a small fee —10c) to the top of the base or you may take the stairs. The former is recommended so that you can save your strength for the heart-pounding climb up a 12-story, 168-step circular staircase to the crown. Here you'll get not only a magnificent view of New York Harbor, but of Liberty, herself, or at least,

Staten Island Ferry — the world's best transporation buy

her arm and torch. The statue's base, incidentally, (formerly Fort Wood), will eventually house the American Museum of Immigration (now under construction) honoring those famous immigrants who came to the United States seeking liberty and opportunity —and found both.

The Statue of Liberty is open daily, including Sundays and holiadys, from 9 a.m. to 5 p.m. —until 6 p.m. with daylight saving time.

Staten Island Ferry

Neighboring the Statue of Liberty Ferry is Big Brother, the Staten Island Ferry, operating for more than a century, and still the best transportation buy in the whole wide world. One almost obsolete nickel will take you on a 20-minute ocean voyage (anyway, the start of one) across the Lower Bay to the St. George terminal on Staten Island. Another insignificant nickel will bring you back. (Cars must pay a stiffer 65c.) En route you'll be given a view second to none of the Lower Manhattan skyline, of Governor's Island, of Liberty Island and its statue and, above all, of New York's bustling harbor with Brooklyn's docks on the left, Newark's on the right and tugs, barges, ships, in short, anything floatable fore and aft, port and starboard.

The ferries shuttle back and forth all day long with arrivals and departures every few minutes during the daylight peak hours. Should the sea air give you an appetite, the ferry's snack bar will take it away if you let it. The Staten Island Ferry, by the way —once it gets moving— is still the most refreshing place to be on a hot August day, air conditioned movies notwithstanding.

State Street Sights

Walking up Whitehall Street from the Staten Island Ferry Terminal, you'll come upon a triangle formed by the intersection of State Street curving into Whitehall. Centered in the green plot stands a flagpole erected to the memory of the first Jewish settlers to come to New York. The year was 1654 and the flagpole speaks much for early New Yorker's religious toleration (reluctantly though it was given) at a time when such a concept was almost unheard of —even by the same colonists who fled their homeland because of religious persecution.

State Street was one of the stateliest of pre-revolutionary days. You'll get some idea of its former grandeur by studying No. 7 State Street, today the home of the Roman Catholic Church of Our Lady of the Rosary. The building was started in 1793 as the residence of a wealthy colonial importer and merchant, James Watson, and in 1808 passed into the hands of an equally wealthy sea captain, Moses Rogers. In 1885 it became the Mission of Our Lady of the Rosary attending to the needs of the swarms of Irish immigrants who fled the Great Famine of 1846 and the subsequent economic depression that followed. By 1928 Irish immigration was at low ebb and the Mission ceased to function as a mission.

Today, the Roman Catholic Church of Our Lady of the Rosary serves the business people of the area. Church though it be, however, its classic Federal-style façade remains pretty much as it was in the elegant days of Messrs. James Watson and Moses Rogers, and though New York is synonomous with change, this is one landmark which will be preserved. Nonetheless, the church itself is in the throes of expansion for Our Lady of the Rosary was recently designated as the seat for the National Shrine of Blessed Mother Seaton, the first American to be beatified by the Roman Catholic Church. Mother Seaton lived at No. 7 State Street from 1801 to 1803.

Walking west on State Street you'll come upon the block-filling Customs House overpowering the corner of State Street and Bowling Green. Outside of its massiveness and its tenants, there's nothing noteworthy about the building itself. Its statues, though, are worth the walk. The four groups at its front, representing Asia, Africa, Europe and America, are the work of Daniel Chester French whom most Americans remember for his remarkable sculpture of the seated Lincoln at the Lincoln Memorial in Washington. The sculptures on the sixth floor represent 12 great commercial centers of the world. Tablets on the Customs House façade claim it completely occupies the site of New York's (or rather, Nieuw Amsterdam's) first fort, Fort Amsterdam, erected in 1626.

Bowling Green

The huge Customs House borders the southern end of Bowling Green, a little patch of verdure best known as the spot —or, at least, near the spot— where Peter Minuit is said to have transacted his famous bargain with the

Reckgawawanck Indians. Bowling Green is also believed to have been the city's first public park though in 1732 it was enclosed and leased to a group of doughty citizens who liked to roll a few games of ten pins on a fine summer's evening and so acquired its name.

Right at Bowling Green, too, is a very famous birthplace —the birthplace of what the early Dutch called the "breede weg." At this point, Broadway starts its erratic course across the whole length of the island. In the days of the colony, Broadway was —for those times— a fine, broad avenue laid out straighter than most. Then it ran up against a stubborn Dutch farmer, Hendrick Brevoort, who wouldn't let the City Fathers cut down a favorite tree —and Broadway took a turn to the west. As the twig is bent. . . . From that moment, Broadway became wayward.

At the north eastern end of Bowling Green, Beaver Street starts on its way to Wall Street. For the thrill of it, walk to the corner of Beaver and Broad. Gaze with awe at the building on the corner —70 Broad. It holds the executive and sales offices of a company that makes more money than any other company in New York City —if not the world: the American Bank Note Co. which prints the bank notes of some 55 to 60 foreign countries. The face value of the bills runs into the billions, one of its officers calculates. The company has been in the business of making money since 1795; used to make it for the United States Government up to the 1870's when the Federal Bureau of Engraving took over the art.

Walk south on Broad. The next "street" —more like an alley— is Marketfield Street which is pretty dull especially since some unimaginative forebearers changed its name. It used to be called Petticoat Lane when the Dutch housewives used it to go to market. Another block will bring you to Stone Street, so called because it was the first street to be paved. Your destination, however, is on the next street —Pearl Street.

Fraunces Tavern

On the southeast corner of Pearl and Broad stands the oldest building in Manhattan, historic Fraunces Tavern, erected in 1719 and a gem of colonial architecture with its balustraded, hipped roof, dormer windows and classic columns at the entrance. Today Fraunces is most remembered as the place where Washington bid a sad but fond farewell of his officers on December 4th, 1783. But it also happens to be the place where the Sons of Liberty met to call for the First Continental Congress and the first meeting place of the oldest existing body of its kind in the United States —the Chamber of Commerce of the State of New York, organized in 1768.

The Tavern was named for Stephan Fraunces, the West Indian proprietor of the Inn, whose cooking was so good, Washington recruited him for his personal steward. The restaurant (occupying the first floor) now specializes in colonial cooking. On the second floor, a museum houses a collection of revolutionary relics and Washingtoniana. The museum is free and open to everyone, but if you want to receive special treatment, take along your school age children. The proprietors seem to feel that the museum is best appreciated by such youngsters. Fraunces Tavern opens weekdays from 10 a.m. to 4 p.m. and Saturdays from 10 a.m. to 3 p.m. It closes Sundays and all holidays —except, of course, Washington's Birthday.

From Fraunces Tavern walk east along Pearl Street until you reach Coenties Slip. Here turn right and walk south on Coenties Slip East. On the way, you'll pass Water Street and Front Street —each at successive times the easternmost limits of Manhattan until the land was filled in— before you reach South Street bordering on the East River. Overhead, on the Franklin Delano Roosevelt (or East River) Drive, automobiles hurry to the Brooklyn-Battery Tunnel or South Ferry and Battery Park. Across the way, New York City's downtown heliport serves the financial district's business men who can afford the best way to avoid the city's incredible traffic snarls.

In its heyday, during the Gold Rush Era, South Street was considered the "Gateway to the West." Its buildings were spruce and trim and along its docks were moored the swift-sailing, history-making clipper ships that contributed much to America's early prosperity. Today South Street is lined, for the most part, with weather-beaten, decaying buildings offering seedy bargains to seamen and destined —it is rumored and devoutly to be wished— to fall victim to the "improvement" rampage presently afflicting New York City. The area between Coenties Slip West and Whitehall will soon be devoured by the proposed new New York Stock Exchange.

Seamen's Church Institute

However, at 25 South Street, on the corner of Coenties Slip East, stands a remarkable institution —the Seamen's Church Institute of New York which started out as a "floating" chapel in 1844 and now has a 13-story headquarters here with additional modern facilities at Newark, New Jersey, and is the world's largest shore center for all merchant seamen who come knocking at its hospitable doors (about a quarter of a million yearly).

Perched on top of the Seamen's Church Institute is one of New York's few lighthouses, a memorial to those who died on the Titanic in the famous disaster of 1912. Also atop the Institute is one of the three remaining time balls in the United States. If you're there around noon you'll be able to see it operate. At 12 p.m. sharp, at a signal from the Naval Observatory in Washington, the hollow, three-foot-in-diameter ball drops —and ships, seamen and knowledgeable pedestrians and motorists traveling along the East River Drive set their watches by it.

Most interesting of all is the Institute's Marine Museum —a really fine one— covering 2000 years of maritime history from reed rafts and viking ships to today's automation on the waves. Admission to the Museum —open daily from 10 a.m. to 6 p.m. except on Christmas and New Year's Day— is free.

A few blocks east of the Institute is Old Slip. Turn left (north) to Hanover Square where stands another landmark —India House, built in 1837 as a private (and very elegant) residence and today a private club catering to private gentlemen with not-so-private interests in foreign commerce. Across from India House, on the north west side of the Square, a plaque commemorates the spot where William Bradford in 1725 started New York City's first newspaper, the *New York Gazette*. The *Gazette* was a loyalist newspaper and —indirectly— did much to further the cause of freedom of the press for its biasness encouraged the start of an opposition paper by John Peter Zenger. Loyalist governor William Crosby had Zenger jailed for libel and then immediately set about disbarring the attorneys attempting to defend him. As a result, Andrew Hamilton, a brilliant young lawyer from Philadelphia was "imported" to defend the newspaper man. Hamilton's impassioned defense not only secured an acquittal for Zenger but was subsequently printed in pamphlet form and distributed and became a classic plea for freedom of the press and liberty.

Walking north on William Street will bring you to one of the world's most famous —or infamous (depending upon your ideology)— streets: Wall Street, a narrow, short canyon of towering banks, trusts and brokerage firms where most of New York City's wealth is concentrated. At the corner of Wall and William Streets (55 Wall) stands —or perhaps floats would be a better description— the First National City Bank, the only building in New York built on quicksand (which may be symbolic of the uncertain nature of wealth). The bank, established in 1812, is an offshoot of the first Bank of the United States founded by a group which included Alexander Hamilton and Aaron Burr.

Federal Hall

One block west, on the corner of Wall and Nassau, stands a national monument —Federal Hall, a striking example of neo-classic architecture. The Hall is dominated by John Quincy Adams Ward's statue of George Washington standing on the front steps approximately on the spot where he took his first inaugural oath. The present Hall was erected in 1842 but it stands on the site where once stood New York City's first City Hall; where John Peter Zenger was tried and acquitted; where the Stamp Act Congress met; where —altered and renamed Federal Hall— the United State's First Congress convened; where the Supreme Court started out life as the guardian of our Constitution; where the Bill of Rights was adopted. A part of this first Federal Hall, incidentally, still exists: a piece of the wrought iron railing from its balcony —the one where Washington took his inaugural oath— was incorporated into the main entrance of Bellevue Hospital at First Avenue and 27th Street.

When the United States capital was moved from New York City to Philadelphia pending the construction of Washington, D.C., old Federal Hall was used to house government offices. The present building first served as the United States Customs House until 1862 when it housed the U.S. Sub-Treasury. Some New Yorkers, in fact, still refer to it as the old Sub Treasury Building though it later became the Federal Reserve Bank of New York. Its role as a National Monument only began on August 11th, 1955 — a timely measure taken, no doubt, to protect it from New York's frenzied building boom. Today Federal Hall houses a museum of early historical relics plus a memorial room dedicated to John Peter Zenger containing an exhibit on the colonies' struggle for freedom of the press.

New York Stock Exchange

Diagonally across from Federal Hall, its dignified, classic exterior belying its internal chaos (at least to the eye), stands that madhouse known as the New York Stock Exchange, the largest securities market in the United States. Guide books delight in telling you how this, New York's first stock exchange, was organized in 1792 by a group of 24 pioneering stalwarts who decided to meet every day under the spreading branches of a buttonwood tree (not too far from the spot where the Exchange now stands) to transact their business of buying and selling stocks. For their trading floor they had a plot of green grass.

Guide books delight in telling you this but they make no attempt to explain the frenetic, apparently directionless activity that occurs daily on the Exchange's floor. This guide book is no different simply because even after a lectured tour of some twenty minutes by an expert guide the situation on the floor still isn't too clear. The net outcome, in any case, is that a fantastic amount of business is conducted on the Exchange's floor and that the lives

Washington looks on the N.Y. Stock Exchange from the steps of Federal Hall

of most (if not all) of us are inextricably entangled in the endless stream of ticker tape spewed by its ticker machines. You may watch the mad scene from a gallery overlooking the trading floor and (highly recommended) take the free guided tours that are conducted Mondays through Fridays from 10 a.m. to 3:30 p.m.

Directly behind Federal Hall, on One Chase Manhattan Plaza, bounded by Nassau, Liberty (in pre-revolutionary days named "Crown Street" and re-named for obviously patriotic reasons), William and Pine Streets, towers Lower Manhattan's recent addition to its skyscraper forest —the striking Chase Manhattan Bank building. The building is unique in several ways. First, it is the only one in the financial district that has anything like elbow-room. Its spacious plaza keeps it isolated and secure from being nudged by other buildings. It's a modern, steel and glass, on-end matchbox-type building of 65 stories, five of which are underground and hold the world's largest bank vault —said to be longer than a football field. It holds some outstanding works of art tastefully scattered hither and yon throughout the building. Free tours of the building are conducted from 9:30 a.m. to 3:30 p.m. by appointment.

Behind the Chase Manhattan Bank, at 33 Liberty Street, is the Federal Reserve Bank of New York, the largest member of the Federal Reserve System. Free tours of this bank of banks are conducted on weekdays at 10, 11 a.m. and 1 and 2 p.m. but *by appointment only.*

Trinity Church

If you look west down Wall Street from Federal Hall you'll be able to see, almost dead center and framed on either side by Wall Street's canyon of skyscrapers, narrow (only 79-feet wide) Trinity Church, one of New York City's most famous landmarks, founded in 1697. The present church completed in 1846 (the third built on the site), is always open and well worth a visit; so is its over-populated graveyard. The church, a not too attractive, neo-Gothic, dirty brownstone structure, has a lovely chapel in the rear, lovely stained glass windows, beautiful bronze bas relief doors —and lovely, lovely money. Trinity Church, in fact, is one of the richest in the world. Queen Anne in 1705 made it a land grant of almost all lower Manhattan. Though the church only retains about one-fifth of its original grant, that still makes it one of New York City's wealthiest landlords —real estate around lower Manhattan going for about $500 the

Narrow Trinity Church framed by Wall Street's canyon of skyscrapers

Apparent bedlam rules supreme on the floor of the New York Stock Exchange

square foot. Columbia University, another wealthy land-lord, (then called Kings College) began its existence in 1754 in a vestry of the church.

The over-crowded cemetery, isolating Trinity Church from the buildings nearby, bears looking into, too. The old tombstones bear such names as Alexander Hamilton, Robert Fulton, William Bradford, etc. Just for curiosity's sake, take a look at the tombstone of an early Mason by the name of James Leeson, buried there in 1794. His epitaph is a cryptographic series of dots. The solution to the cryptogram, published in the Trinity Record about a century later, works out to "Remember Death," but why this sage advice is given cryptographically no one has been able to explain.

Another interesting point the New York Convention & Visitors Bureau is quick to point out: the first tomb of the Unknown Soldier isn't in the Arlington National Cemetery but in Trinity's graveyard where the "Martyrs' Monument" marks the burial place of some unknown colonial soldiers who died aboard the British prison ships anchored in New York's harbor during the Revolution.

American Stock Exchange

Behind Trinity Church, at 86 Trinity Place, the American Stock Exchange, largest market for foreign securities in the United States and second largest securities market, holds its own orderly chaos. Originally it was known as the New York Curb exchange because its first meeting place (prior to the Civil War) was a curb on Wall Street near Hanover Street. Later the outdoor traders in securities shifted their base of operations to the front of the Mills Building on Broad Street. If night caught them still trading, they would retire to the corridors of uptown hotels where business was carried on as usual.

The Exchange finally acquired a roof over its head (and regular trading hours) in the early 1900's but only changed its name to the American Stock Exchange in 1953. Again, you may watch the whole mess from the visitor's gallery open from 10 a.m. to 3:30 p.m., Mondays through Fridays or see a film or hear a lecture on the stock exchange up until 3 p.m. and there's no change for this inside track on what seems like sheer lunacy.

If by now you're footsore and weary, hop the BMT local near the American Stock Exchange for one stop to the north exit of the Cortland Street station. To the west, an area bounded by Liberty Street on the south, West Street, Vesey and Barclay Streets on the north and Church Street (where you are standing) on the east has been earmarked for the proposed 16-acre World Trade Center of the New York Port of Authority. The present plans call for the construction on this site of the two tallest buildings in the world, twin towers designed to look down on the 1250-foot Empire State Building from their height of 1350 feet. Work is scheduled to begin in 1965 and be completed five year —and $350 million— later.

St. Paul's Church

A walk of one block north and another east will bring you to St. Paul's Chapel at Broadway and Fulton Street, the oldest church in New York City. Built in 1776, the church is a charming example of Georgian architecture. Its barrel vaulting, white walls and sparkling crystal chandeliers will give you a feeling of spaciousness and airiness despite its small size. George Washington attended Sunday services regularly at St. Paul's Chapel and a "G" and the U.S. Coat of Arms marks the pew in the north aisle where he used to kneel to worship.

West of St. Paul's, at 228 Fulton Street (unless it

has already been dispossessed by the proposed World Trade Center) thrives the nationally known Trefflich Bird and Animal Co., Inc. which, besides having a fascinating pet department, supplies inmates for zoos throughout the United States. If you have children in tow, this is certainly the place to take them. You are entirely welcome to come in and browse. However, you may find yourself digging deep into your pocket for an irresistible piece of merchandise.

Across the way from St. Paul's, at 222 Broadway, stands one of New York City's newer buildings, the home of the Western Electric Co. Some New Yorkers with nostalgic grandfathers will remember this corner best because it was once occupied by P. T. Barnum's American Museum (which he bought in 1841) where thousands of New Yorkers and foreign visitors flocked to see, among other freakish wonders, "General Tom Thumb," the diminutive dwarf, Charles Stratton, who at his tallest height measured only 31 inches.

At the corner of Ann and Broadway, too, you'll find the start of Park Row, once Newspaper Row, that exciting street where all New York City's newspapers were gathered and where news was, if not made, written. The only thing remaining from those glamorous days is the old *Tribune Tower,* New York's first "skyscraper."

Fulton Fish Market

Clear across town from St. Paul's at South and Fulton Streets —your nose will direct you— the famous (and odoriferous) Fulton Fish Market exudes its aura of the sea and fish. Alas, like so many other picturesque (if seedy) parts of New York City, the market is in its last agony for the area has been slated for improvement. If you want to see and smell this dying institution, this

The morning's catch is unloaded at the Fulton Fish Market

is your last chance. To see it best, though, you'll have to be an early riser. An unbelievable bustle of activity starts at about 3 o'clock in the morning but by 8 or 9 o'clock the market is almost as dead as the fish it sells, for all good fish (fresh) should be in the freezing compartments of the city's markets by that time.

Section	From City Hall to Greenwich Village.
Map	See page 74.
First stop	BMT (via tunnel) to City Hall — local stop; IRT-Lexington Avenue to Brooklyn Bridge-Worth Street (City Hall) — express stop; IRT-Seventh Avenue to Park Place (Broadway) — express stop.
Where to eat	Chinese Rathskeller, Eberlin's, Grotto Azzurra, Joe King's German-American Rathskeller, Joy Young, Moskowitz & Lupowitz, Shavey Lee's Tung Sai, Stanley Chin's Tai Yat Low, Teddy's.
Sights for the children	Chinatown and the Chinatown Museum.

4

From Riches to Rags

The 'solid gold front'
of the financial district
and lower Manhattan as seen
from the Empire State Building

The turn of the 19th century found New York City a bustling town of perhaps 50,000 almost entirely concentrated around the tip of lower Manhattan in an area not much larger than five square miles. Lower Broadway, State Street, Pearl Street, Stone Street —these were the grand streets. The chaos and depression that had gripped the country at the end of the Revolutionary War had been curbed. People everywhere were mending their fences but New York, especially prosperous, was not only mending but building new ones to accommodate the many newcomers the prospects of wealth and prosperity were attracting to her gates.

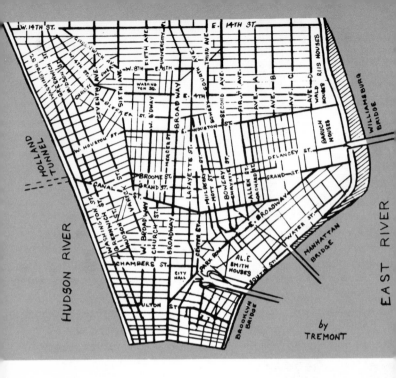

by
TREMONT

City Hall Park and City Hall

So, the City Fathers started thinking of building a new City Hall to replace the one converted into Federal Hall, when, for a brief spell, New York had been the capital of the young nation. The town's Commons, they decided, on the fringe of town, would be a most appropriate site for the new Hall. Here on the Commons —today City Hall Park, the triangular green patch of land starting at Park Row and extending to Chambers Street— the Sons of Liberty had erected liberty poles (the first was on June 4th, 1766) just about as fast as the British had cut them down. (This colonial diversion finally stopped with the erection of a liberty pole inscribed "Liberty and Property" apparently a sentiment agreeable to both factions.) Here the Declaration of Independence had been read in the presence of George Washington and to an exultant audience.

The city was growing quickly, the City Fathers reasoned, and no doubt would soon reach the site proposed for the new Hall. Just beyond the Commons, however, lay a large marshy area and pond —Collect Pond where, in 1796, John Fitch had tried out models of his new invention, the steamboat. Extending beyond it, the Bouwerie cut a path through green countryside to the huge Stuyvesant farm and chapel, St. Mark's-in-the-Bouwerie. It wasn't likely, the City Fathers continued to reason, that the city would jump the pond and expand further north. So they contracted the services of the brilliant architectural firm of Mangin and McComb and in 1803 lay the cornerstone for their new City Hall. Half a million dollars —a fantastic amount for those days— was spent on its construction for the city hall of such an up and coming town as New York had to be outstanding.

When City Hall was completed in 1812, it more than filled the greatest expectations. The building was (and still is) a jewel of governmental architecture, a building which moved Lafayette's secretary to write that it was the only building in New York worth looking at, a building which, in fact, has served as the model for many other city halls of small communities. The Hall, designed in the style of Louis XVI, was faced with marble at the front and sides, but the frugal City Fathers, having decided that the city was not likely to go beyond the Pond, saw no reason to waste costly marble on the rear exterior (which not many would be likely to see) and so they left the back in brownstone.

Today City Hall looks just as good as new —if not better. The present administration recently made up for the penny-wise, pound-foolish Knickerbockers of 1812.

City Hall underwent a complete overhauling: front and side marble was cleaned and repaired —and marble added to the rear. The cost of the restoration work was about $12 million —four times as much as it had originally cost to construct City Hall. The consensus is that this architectural gem is well worth it. (In contrast, costing more than six times as much, the City Court Building stands, not far from the Hall, as a monument to graft —and indifferent taste. But more of that in its proper place.)

Underneath the Hall's dome, an exquisite staircase with one branch curving to the right and the other to the left leads you to the "Governor's Suite" (now a museum) where you may see the desks used by the first three presidents of the United States, plus some portraits by American artists and other historical memorabilia. The museum (free) is open on weekdays only from 10 a.m. to 5 p.m.

City Hall Park has its points of interest, too. On the west stands a bound Nathan Hale, looking proud and defiant, as he must have looked when he regretted he had only one life to give for his country. On the east stands an affable Ben Franklin, in the role of printer and newspaper man —a gentle reminder that New York is the center of America's printing and publishing industry.

In the park, too, stands a replica of one of those poles the rebellious Sons of Liberty were wont to put up on the town Commons. But these revolutionary activities are far behind it. Today the Park provides the setting for the welcoming ceremonies for visiting V.I.P.'s and other special civic events, while City Hall only houses the offices of the Mayor, the President of the City Council, the Art Commission and the meeting rooms of the City Council and the Board of Estimates. The other municipal departments long since outgrew the beautiful but limited accommodations of the Hall (not much larger than those private

residences built in the heydays of the Astors, the Vanderbilts, the Goulds, the Belmonts, etc.). These departments
now tenant the municipal office buildings (on Foley
Square behind the Park where Collect Pond once used
to be) which tower over City Hall but in no way over-
shadow it.

One of these buildings is the "Tweed" City Court
Building at 52 Chambers Street whose chief claim to fame
is in its cost. More than $12 million of New York City
taxpayers' money went to erect this building —more,
someone has calculated, than what it cost to build
London's Houses of Parliament— and 75% of that
amount went to enrich the bank accounts of the already
graft-rich Tammany-controlling Tweed Ring. The City
Court Building, nonetheless, may have been cheap at the
price. It indirectly led to the downfall of "Boss" William
Marcy Tweed, who had controlled Tammany Hall for
more than 10 years, and to the breaking up of the "Tweed
Ring" which had kept New York City virtually under a
complete dictatorship for almost 30 months. During the
interim, the Ring plundered New York City taxpayers of
a conservatively estimated $45 million.

Woolworth Building

The Tweed City Court Building for a long time
symbolized monumental graft; the building almost directly
south, on the other side of the park, for a long time
symbolized monumental height. At 233 Broadway, near
the southern tip of City Hall Park, towers the 60-story
Woolworth building erected in 1913. For 17 years it held
the title of the world's tallest office building until the
Chrysler Building appeared on the scene and stole the
honors. Despite its age, the Woolworth Building is still
one of the most handsome of New York. For the best

look at the skyscraper, cross to the other side of the Park where you may have an almost unobstructed view without having to lie on the sidewalk and look up.

Brooklyn Bridge

Here on the east side of City Hall Park begin the approaches to one of New York City's most loved and maligned landmarks: the venerable yet charming Brooklyn Bridge. When it was first opened to the public in 1883, it was an engineering wonder —the longest suspension span in the world— which the chronic pessimists predicted wouldn't stand up for long. Almost a century later, all prettied and modernized and moreover, carrying many times its original load, Brooklyn Bridge like City Hall is as good if not better than the days when, as New York City's latest novelty, it became a favorite jumping off spot for suicides. A pedestrian walk will take you across the bridge to the Brooklyn side and offers one of the loveliest views of Manhattan. It is especially beautiful at sundown with the lights of lower Manhattan's skyscrapers starting to gleam and the tall, dark buildings silhouetted against a sky streaked with amber and rose. The city, incidentally, makes some money on Brooklyn Bridge by leasing storage and work space inside the bridge's arches. In fact, even before the bridge was open to the public, its arch vaults served as wine cellars. One historical note: the bridge stands on the site where the first "white house" used to be —1-3 Cherry Street, Washington's home while New York City was capital of the United States.

The Lower East Side

North of Brooklyn Bridge sprawled one of New York's most slum-ridden, crime-ridden neighborhoods —the Lower East Side, an area extending roughly from

City Hall Park to just below 14th Street, from just east of Broadway to the East River. Strangely enough, in earlier days, this had been one of the most idyllic and elite sections of the city. Then along came progress: a canal was built to drain Collect Pond, incidentally giving birth to Canal Street. The pond and the marshy land surrounding the pond —which probably had contributed much to the epidemics of yellow fever and small pox that had ravaged the city during the late 18th and early 19th century— were filled. More fine homes were built and more of the elite (and *nouveau riche*) flocked to this fashionable section of New York.

The land, however, remained marshy and the houses deteriorated and were abandoned by their high society owners who once again moved north —this time to Greenwich Village and lower Fifth Avenue. When the waves of immigrants began pounding the shores of New York, they first settled in the Lower East Side. The area became an international clearinghouse of the poor, the huddled masses —and of stolen goods. Absentee land-lordism was the order of the day and the houses became vermin- and rat-infested. In fact, one of the more innocent sports of the Lower East Side were the "rat fights" in which a terrier would be pitted against a cage of hungry, ferocious rats.

The Bouwerie (now the Bowery) —that once lovely wide lane leading to the Stuyvesant farm— had become the center of the theater and entertainment world —and the center of crime and vice, a combination the police not only tolerated but actively encouraged. They found it a lucrative business to offer their "protection" to the brothels and saloons lining the narrow strip. The Bowery was the domain of a famous gang —the Bowery Boys— a bunch of hoodlums, far from boyish, with a definite social status in their neighborhood which they maintained with a select arsenal of weapons —brass knuckles, lead pipes, knives, guns.

Row upon row of crumbling, moldy houses lined the section east of the Bowery and along the East River. Here families of four, five, six, even more, lived, ate and slept in one slime-covered room. Along the streets the Irish brogue intermingled with the German guttural and the softer sounds of Russian, Polish, Yiddish, Italian. . . . each compartmentalized in a tight section of four or five streets.

In recent years, progress has again caught up with the Lower East Side. Much of the squalor has given place to modern housing developments looking out upon the river —the Alfred E. Smith, Corlears Hook, Bernard Baruch, Lillian Wald, Jacob Riis developments offer homes for low and middle income groups. Parks, playgrounds, an athletic field have replaced the horrors that once edged the waterfront. With the Third Avenue El gone, sunlight now brightens the dark and dingy —and once dangerous— corners of New York's seedy back yard.

The Bowery

Today the Bowery is still the tramping grounds of the destitute, the panhandlers, the prostitutes and the social workers —but their days there are numbered. Too much light pains alcohol-bleared eyes. The decrepit buildings are slowly being transformed into modern dwellings offering little comfort or dark corners where a wino can sleep off a drunk until it's time again for the day's first libation.

There are still flophouses where the Bowery-rich can find a bed (of sorts) for $1.00. You'll find shops where men's suits go for $7.95; haircuts for 10c. Some spots still serve three 6½ oz. glasses of wine for one round quarter (if you get there between 8 and 10 a.m.) and breakfast for 20c. You'll find these places always jammed at that time. Even before opening time, a ragged line forms waiting to get in —waiting for the artificial courage to see them through the day. They shuffle in these men with watery eyes, unsteady hands, cotton in their mouths, and elbow to elbow at the bar, they lean over to sip the top off their first glass. (Unsteady hands can't raise the glass without spilling.) Later, after the worst part of the day is over, they'll hang around in small ragged bunches to chat and pass the time of day.

The Bowery Brethren don't worry too much about the weather —not at all about the world situation. But with some a big worry is starting to gnaw at the back of their minds. Where are they going to go when "progress" really hits the Bowery?

Most New Yorkers rarely go to the Bowery. They don't even have a clear idea of where it is. Most think of it as a rather large lump of lower Manhattan teeming with filth, empty wine bottles and human dregs. Actually, it's a fairly narrow strip arising at Chatham Square (where Park Row ends) and extending for some 15 blocks or so to Cooper Square. It is the dividing line between Chinatown and Little Italy on the west and what, for many years, was New York's solid Jewish district on the east.

Along Orchard and Delancey Streets —the traditional Jewish shopping center— you'll still find pushcart markets and long lines of booth-like shops crammed with anything from gefulte fish to ear muffs and you'll find they do an especially brisk business on Sundays. But, today there are signs that read *"ropas para hombres y mujeres"* (clothes for men and women) mingled with the kosher signs and the local grocer sells *plátanos* (plantains) along

The traditional Jewish shopping centers along Orchard and Delancey Streets on the Lower East Side now also cater to a newcomer ...

... the Puerto Rican. Note the partly visible signs in Spanish: 'Para hombres y niños' and 'para mujeres' —'for men and boys; for women'

with lox and bagels for Puerto Rican newcomers have invaded this Jewish stronghold.

In this, too, New York is changing. Education, opportunities, circumstances, but mostly time have blurred the sharp demarcation lines that once divided the various foreign section of the city. The children born of these ghettos leave to go to school or get jobs and return with amalgamated ideas —sometimes with wives and husbands and the amalgamation is propagated.

Chinatown

Education, time, progress, though, seem to have no effect on the section of some seven blocks or so just north west of Chatham Square —Chinatown. Some 6000 Chinese live in this tight little community along Mott, Pell, Doyer, Elizabeth and Canal Streets —and another 40,000 come to do their shopping and visit with their cousins. True, with the El down, you can no longer expect to find an opium den in its shadows. The Tong Wars of yesterday are as dead as a chess game played by correspondence.

Nonetheless, the mysterious Orient still lurks around Chinatown's corners. You'll find Chinese restaurants serving authentic Chinese food —not the chow mein and chop suey of the Occidental— and Chinese groceries offering all the exotic ingredients that go into its making. Shops cram the streets selling all kinds of Oriental wares —some authentic, some made in Brooklyn. You may even step inside a Chinese temple and buy souvenirs in front of an oversized Buddha.

Strangely enough an Occidental drugstore at 6 Bowery (between Doyer and Pell Streets) —the Oliffe Drug Store— the oldest in continuous operation in the United States (at the present address since 1805), does a brisk business in leaches and ginseng root with its Oriental customers.

If you decide to eat in one of Chinatown's innumerable restaurants, pick one that has a preponderantly Chinese clientele —and not one catering to American tourists— to taste authentic Mandarin and Cantonese dishes and to admire (but don't stare, please) at the dexterity of your fellow diners as they manipulate two chopsticks better than you can manipulate a fork.

Don't expect to find venerable, bearded Chinese elders in silk embroidered kimonos walking the streets of Chinatown —the ceremonial robes are reserved for state occasions such as the "'eye-opening" ceremonies of a new "lion" for the Chinese New Year or the Chinese New Year itself. Then "lions" —fierce paper maché animals glorious to behold rage in the streets while Mon Jong (Ten Thousand Firecrackers) explode noisily at their feet and all Chinatown is dressed up and as Oriental as can be. If you happen to be in New York in the "Season of the Great Snow and of the Great Cold," but before the "Season of the Rain Waters," when the "white moon of the winter solstice has faded and the bitter moon of the 12th month is gone" (i.e., a movable date usually in February but perhaps in late January or early March), then by all means go to Chinatown and watch the Chinese welcome the Year of the Serpent (1965 —but as the Chinese count, 4663). This year (1964) they're celebrating the Year of the Dragon and for 365 days they will pray and make burnt offerings to the dragon —for the Chinese consider it a sacred animal deity responsible for the rain and thus for lush harvests, prosperity and peace.

If you want to learn more about Chinese culture and customs, go to the Chinatown Museum at 7 Mott

Chinatown lions
romp in the streets
on the Chinese
New Year while
a Chinese market
offers exotic
Chinese ingredients
all year long

Street where you'll find all sorts of displays on China and the Chinese including exhibitions of flowers and fruits native to China and what they symbolize to the Chinese, Chinese printing and music (with color sound film), Chinese coins and even Chinese chopsticks. The museum is open daily (at least, for 364 days of the year) from 10 a.m. to 10 p.m., unless by special arrangement, and offers a printed tour of Chinatown to its visitors.

Admission: Children (i.e., anyone under 18) at all times, 25c. Adults—weekdays, 35c; Sat., Sun. and holidays, 50c.

Little Italy

North of Chinatown in that section of New York known as "Little Italy" (with Mulberry Street its capital) walk the *compare* and *comare* and other *paesani* of that joyous breed. (You'll find others around Bleecker Street on the fringes of Greenwich Village to the north.) The shops are adorned with strings of *provalone* and Italian sausages and the wonderful, wonderful smell of spices and rich Italian food.

To see Little Italy at its most charming —and exuberant— come when the Italians are celebrating the feast day of San Gennaro (occurring in mid-September), the patron saint of the Neapolitans. You'll find Mulberry Street transformed into a little Naples with an arcade of intricately designed arches with colored lights, singing and dancing in the streets, stall upon stall offering anything from *antipasto* to *zeppole* and, presiding over all, the statue of San Gennaro garbed in feast-day best and decorated with dollar bills pinned to his robes by grateful (or would be) beneficiaries of his intercession. The Italians celebrate other feast days but none as uproariously as San Gennaro's. Admission to this carnival-like street scene is free. Everyone is welcome and the cost of sampling at the stalls is so reasonable that you will find that your wallet is growing leaner, yourself growing fatter, almost imperceptibly as the evening wears on —but the feast day of San Gennaro occurs only once a year, so enjoy it.

To the southeast, a road branching off Canal Street takes you to the Manhattan Bridge, opened to traffic in 1909, the third bridge to cross the East River to Brooklyn. Northeast, the Schiff Parkway (Delancey Street) leads to the Williamsburg Bridge, completed in 1903, second bridge to span the East River.

The Holland Tunnel

Across town, on the western end of Canal Street, lies the Holland Tunnel, the first to burrow its way across the Hudson River to 12th and 14th streets in Jersey City. When the tunnel was opened to traffic in November of 1927, it was another of the world's wonders —a pioneer engineering feat which still serves as the basis for other vehicular tunnels throughout the world. The tunnel, in fact, is named after the pioneering engineer —Clifford M. Holland— who solved the engineering problems which had previously been obstacles to such a project. Chief of these was the problem of ventilating such a long (approximately 8500 feet) tunnel. If you go down to the Hudson River by Canal Street, you will see four buildings —two on either side of the river by the tunnel. They house gigantic fans which keep changing the air every 90 seconds. So far New York's Port of Authority has invested some $60 million on the Holland Tunnel —recently $2½ million to speed the dispersal of traffic into lower Manhattan streets. The investment has been well worth it: in recent times, yearly traffic through the Holland Tunnel has amounted to more than 21 million vehicles paying at least the 50c toll charged passenger cars.

Out for lunch in Greenwich Village

Section	Greenwich Village to 32nd Street.
Map	See page 90.
First stop	IND to West 4th Street — express stop; BMT to 8th Street — local stop; IRT-Lexington Avenue to Astor Place — local stop; IRT-Broadway, Seventh Avenue to Christopher Street-Sheridan Square (local stop).
Where to eat	Albert French, Balkan Armenian, Captain's Table, Cavanagh's The Coach House, Dardanelles Armenian, Felix's, Hearthstone, Jai Alai, the Lichee Tree, Limelight, Lüchow's, Mandarin House, McSorley's Old Ale House, Mona Lisa, O. Henry's Steak House, Per Bacco, Seventeen Barrow, Steuben House.
Sights for the children	Greenwich Village spring and autumn outdoor art show, Old Merchant's Home, Theodore Roosevelt Memorial Home.

5

Vanishing Bohemia

Governor Wouter Van Twiller started the trend northward back in the 1630's when he bought some land from the Indians two miles or so north of Nieuw Amsterdam. The fires and primarily the epidemics that emaciated lower Manhattan in the 1700's and 1800's hastened the population movement to the idyllic hamlet outside the city. By the 1850's Greenwich Village (as the hamlet came to be known) was unquestionably the domain of the Select —though the Bohemians (including the shocking Walt Whitman) were already beginning to gnaw at its fringes.

Real Bohemia did not awaken the sleepy village until the 1910's —Eugene O'Neill, Max Eastman, Edna St. Vincent Millay, Floyd Dell, Willa Cather, Edwin Arlington Robinson, Theodore Dreiser were among the "alarm clocks." Others, attracted by the prospects of intellectual stimulation (a commodity very much at a premium), came to visit often —Amy Lowell,. Sherwood Anderson. Before long the doings of this part of town became a source of national pride —and national scandal. And before long those who wanted to be different merely for the sake of being different —and being in the spot-

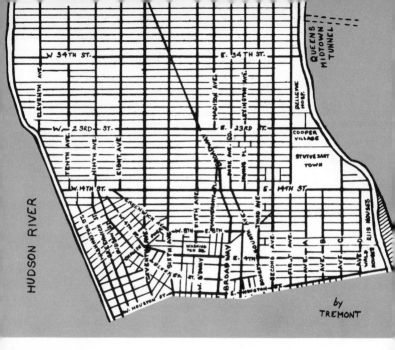

light— started invading the Village. So did those who wanted to be different merely to cash in on the tourist trade.

The intellectuals tolerated the nuts for a time but when the tourists began arriving and —worse still— couldn't tell the difference between them, the death knell for the Village as an avant-garde artistic center was sounded. Intellectual stimulation, alas, deserted the Village —deserted New York City altogether, the bitter claim.

Greenwich Village

Today what mostly lingers in that notorious area (bounded by 13th Street in the north, by Broadway in the east, by Bleeker Street on the south and by Hudson Street on the west) is The Greenwich Village Legend, a collection of beatniks trying to be different but afraid of leaving the sheltering confines of their circle for fear they won't "belong," some slim-flanked "boys" in tight pants and husky-voiced "girls" in suits —and some of the most respectable families in New York City trying desperately to preserve their cherished Village from the building ague that has given the whole town the shivers. Thanks to the latter, progress has been slow in arriving and you will find that Greenwich Village has some of the most charming streets and sections of Manhattan with the earlier homes dating back to the 1820's. You'll also find that it has some excellent restaurants, a few good nightclubs and some café expresso shops where the beatniks play checkers or chess while the tourists watch wide-eyed and where the coffee is generally excellent (if you like café expresso and its infinite varieties) and the pastries delicious.

▪ Washington Square

The heart of the Village is Washington Square, in early colonial days the city's Potter's Field and Gallows Hill but today the *de facto* campus of New York University, the Square's most important landlord and the largest privately financed educational institution in the world. Though the University, located in seven centers throughout New York City, consists of 15 separate schools and colleges, nine of these are at Washington Square and many of the buildings lining the Square are school buildings and other facilities used by the University center's 25,000 students. Recent additions to the scene are the outstanding Loeb Student Center at West Broadway and Washington Square South and the spanking new residence hall for men and women at University and Waverly Place. Communications history was made on the Square, by the way. Prof. Samuel F. B. Morse perfected his telegraph in the building where stands 100 Washington Square East.

In the center of the tree-shaded Square, a large fountain and pool attract students, beatniks, residents and visitors on fine Sunday afternoons. Students and beatniks come to hear themselves sing folksongs accompanying themselves on guitars, residents come to enjoy the sun and visitors come to enjoy both. Several years ago, then Park Commissioner Robert Moses —probably on the petition of some residents who found all the available seats in the sun occupied once too often— tried to ban the folk singers on the grounds that they constituted a public disturbance. The uproar was instantaneous —25,000 students (and some residents) rallied 'round the cause of Freedom of Expression. As you may surmise, the folksinging and guitar playing go on as usual.

■ Washington Arch

Dominating the northern face of the Square is the imposing, classic Washington Arch built in 1895 to replace an earlier provisional arch which had been erected to commemorate the centennial of Washington's inauguration. New York City's noted architect Stanford White, who left his artistic mark hither and yon throughout Manhattan, designed this beautiful arch. Unarchitecturally minded New Yorkers, however, probably remember him best as the alleged (as the newspapers put it) lover who was killed by a jealous husband (Harry Kendall Thaw) over the "Girl on the Red Velvet Swing" (Evelyn Nesbit —a chorus girl in the famed Floradora review).

Washington stands in duplicate —on one side as a civilian, on the other as a soldier— at the north face of the Arch looking unpreturbed on the birth of that famous avenue —Fifth.

Just above the Arch, between Washington Square North and 8th Street, are two of the most charming streets

'Meet me at the fountain in Washington Square'

in all of New York City looking very much like something out of Victorian London: Washington Mews (east of Fifth Avenue) and McDougal Alley (west of Fifth, but with its entrance off McDougal Street). Both were once the alleys leading to the stables and carriage houses of New York's wealthy in the days when owning horses and carriages were *de riguer*. Both stables and carriage houses have been converted into studios —wealthy Gertrude Vanderbilt Whitney (who liked to try her hand at sculpturing and who founded the Whitney Museum of American Art) started the fashion in the early part of this century and others quickly followed.

■ Old Merchant's Home

One block north at 29 East 4th Street, just east of Broadway, stands another ghost from the past —the Old Merchant's House, built in 1830 and once the residence of wealthy merchant Seabury Tredwell. The last person to live in this fine old house —an unaltered example of the Federal Period with its arched entrance flanked by a classic column on either side— was the merchant's spinster daughter Gertrude who was born, lived and died there in 1933 at the age of 93.

The house is exactly as it was then, its exterior a little more weatherbeaten perhaps but inside preserving the old fashion elegance in which Miss Gertrude Tredwell lived. You'll see her four-poster bed, the Duncan Phyfe furniture, the Dutch Oven and long-handled bread toaster, her dainty, outmoded wardrobe and even the books this lonely recluse read —"True Politeness," "Etiquette for Ladies" and the old family Bible.

Admission to this memorial to past gentility is 50c —unless you happen to be a New York Public School student. In that case you'll be admitted free. The house is open weekdays (except Monday) from 11 a.m. to 5 p.m. and Sundays and holidays from 1 p.m. to 5 p.m. It shuts its doors Mondays, Christmas and all during August.

North of the Old Merchant's House, between Broadway and Lafayette Street, just below 8th Street, is Astor Place, once citadel of the John Jacob Astor Astors. Later, when entertainment (ever the follower of High Society) moved north, it became the site of the Astor Place Opera House —and the scene of one of New York City's most incredible riots. The rumpus was started over the artistic rivalry between English actor William Charles Macready and American actor Edwin Forrest. When the rumble was over some 20 people were dead and hundreds injured.

■ Cooper Union

Just east of Astor Place, round about Cooper Square, stands Cooper Union for the Advancement of

Science and Art, a group of buildings which are a monument to one man's dream and enlightened philanthropy. Peter Cooper filled a lifelong ambition when in 1859 he established Cooper Institute. Cooper, a self-made industrialist and inventor, the builder of America's first locomotive, "The Tom Thumb," was determined to provide those with ability a free education regardless of race, color, creed or social position —an opportunity which had been denied him. He devoted his life to amassing a fortune for this purpose, dedicated Cooper Union to it and in his will provided for its perpetuation. Today the only entrance requirement for Cooper Union continues to be ability.

The institute also continues to present in its Great Hall (the largest auditorium in New York City when it was built) the free forums which Peter Cooper had envisioned as a sounding board for enlightened ideas. The forums became nationally famous overnight when, on February 27th, 1860, Lincoln delivered his stirring pre-nomination speech voicing his opposition to the extension of slavery and his plea to preserve the Union. Though rioters shouted outside the building and though Lincoln was hanged in effigy from the mast of ships anchored in the harbor, this speech —as Lincoln later put it— "made me President." The Great Hall has heard many other speeches since then, but none has had the impact or the far-reaching effects of Lincoln's Cooper Union Address.

Nonetheless, several events at the Great Hall have changed the course of New York City's history: on September 30th, 1871, the campaign to overthrow the Tweed Ring was launched at a citizens' mass meeting in the Hall; 62 years later Fiorello La Guardia launched his own (successful) campaign against Tammany Hall. Incidentally, today's speakers continue to use the same lectern that Lincoln used on the occasion of his history-making speech.

The Cooper Union Forum is presented at the Great Hall on Mondays, Wednesdays and Fridays, from October through March, starting at 8:30 p.m. Lectures by nationally known speakers are presented on Mondays and Wednesdays, and on Fridays, programs of dance, music and drama. No admission is charged to any of these programs.

The Foundation Building of Cooper Union (which was recently made a National Historic Landmark) also houses the unique Cooper Union Museum for the Arts of Decoration with exhibits on rare textiles from the 3rd Century B.C. to the present, plus drawings, prints, paintings, ceramics, metalwork, wallpapers, furniture, etc. —in short, anything to do with the decorative arts. The museum is used as a center for research in design and applied arts by professionals as well as students but is also open to the public (free of charge) daily, except Sundays, from 10 a.m. to 5 p.m.

▪ St. Marks-in-the-Bouwerie

Just north east of Cooper Square at Second Avenue and 10th Street stands another landmark —old St. Marks-in-the-Bouwerie. The original chapel was built by Peter Stuyvesant in 1660 on the edge of his huge farm, but the present picturesque little church dates from 1799. Among the notables buried in its churchyard are Peter Stuyvesant, himself, and Commodore Matthew C. Perry. You'll find a rather unconvential stain glass window on its north wall —a portrait of its peg-legged founder.

▪ Grace Church

Two blocks west of St. Marks-in-the-Bouwerie at 10th Street and Broadway, its delicate Gothic spire piercing the sky stands Grace Church probably the most fashionable church of the mid-19th century. Built in 1846, it was designed in the neo-Gothic style that was the fad those days by architect James Renwick who later went uptown to design St. Patrick's Cathedral. (The urn standing in the garden, though, isn't Gothic. It's Roman from Nero's time.)

So fashionable was Grace Church at one time that among the prerequisites to being a member of High Society —according to the editor of society's fashionable *The Home Journal*— were "keeping a carriage, living above Bleecker Street, going to Grace Church. . . ."

Not only did anyone who was anybody go to Grace Church to be married or buried, but they also called upon its sexton, Isaac Brown, to make such momentous decisions as to who should be on the invitation list for weddings and funerals as well as other less spiritual dinner parties and balls. With that decided, he would advise who to select as caterer, florist, where to place the orchestra, etc. In short, Sexton Brown saw not only to the Elect's spiritual but to their social welfare. He was, in fact, High Society's social arbiter —the Delphic oracle of the Right People— but he was not without his lighter moments. The lenten season is dull, he once admitted, ". . . but we manage to make our funerals as entertaining as possible."

Occasionally, though, Grace Church had time for lesser folk: with his usual showmanship, P. T. Barnum had his two main attractions —the diminutive Tom Thumb and even more diminutive Lavinia Warren married at Grace Church. It was the wedding of the year.

Fashion —such as the skyscraper apartment at 2 Fifth Avenue— has hit the Village and much of its quaintness on the east side is gone. For the old world atmosphere you'll have to go west of Fifth Avenue in Greenwich Village and walk along the small winding streets, laid out without rhyme or reason thanks, probably, to the yellow fever epidemics which drove hundreds of panicked New

Yorkers from lower Manhattan into the bucolic sterility of a country hamlet. Here you'll find the iron grillwork, the enclosed shady courts, the ancient, outdated gaslamps on their posts by the door, the brass knockers that give this west part of the Village its 19th century manners. One of the streets at the northwest corner of Greenwich Village, incidentally, was named Bank Street because of the banks which fled epidemic-stricken lower Manhattan and set up shop along here.

■ Sheridan Square

South of West 10th Street along Sheridan Square and its periphery —Waverly Place, Washington Place, Fourth Avenue, Grove Street, Christopher Street —are located most of the Village's *intime* nightclubs, cafés and restaurants, some of them weird, some of them with excellent floor shows, but none rating as the dens of iniquity which most out-of-towners expect to find.

■ Grove Court

Southwest of Sheridan Square, between Bedford and Hudson Streets, in quiet introspection, stands a group of six 3-story homes centered around a brick courtyard entered from Grove Street through an ancient iron gate. This is Grove Court —beloved of the Villagers and looking much as it did back in the first half of the 19th century when the Village was still very much of a quiet country hamlet and the Court was known as Pig's Alley and Mixed Ale Alley. Most of houses rest on foundations laid down by the early Knickerbockers and in fact some bear the traces of the old Dutch ovens the *hausfraus* used.

According to a legend, O. Henry placed the setting of his short story, "The Last Leaf," in quiet, unchanging Grove Court. Another legend —but there's an old newspaper clipping to substantiate this one— claims that a city sound survey rated the Court as having the lowest decibel count in Manhattan. Even today this isn't too hard to believe once you've stepped through the ancient gate.

■ St. Luke's Chapel

At Hudson and Grove Streets quietly stands charming old St. Luke's Chapel —known as St. Luke's-in-the-Field back in 1822 when the Village was still all meadows watered by gurgling Minetta Stream. (Minetta has since gone underground, covered by building foundations, but it pops up in the oddest places —the lobby of the tall apartment building at 2 Fifth Avenue, for example, in the guise of a fountain.) St. Luke's once had a now-famous warden, Clement C. Moore, who started a poem with the immortal line, " 'Twas the night before Christmas . . ."— and delighted children ever since. Warden Moore was buried in St. Luke's churchyard but in 1882 he and 699 others were transferred to the graveyard at 155th Street and Broadway.

■ 75½ Bedford

Bedford Street, around the corner from Grove Court, has the distinction of having the narrowest house in New York City —No. 75½— a mere 9½ feet wide. John Barrymore and Edna St. Vincent Millay once lived there —at different times of course.

■ Cherry Lane Theater

Southwest at 38 Commerce Street stands the Village's famous Cherry Lane Theater, a converted barn where aspiring productions are staged by aspiring producers and played by aspiring actors. Some of these productions are really excellent and you would do well to check the entertainment pages of New York's newspapers and magazines to see if anything is currently playing.

North of Greenwich Village, extending from river to river, runs 14th Street, one of New York's main if rather shoddy looking crosstown thoroughfares. It is generally crammed with trucks, buses, cars, shops of all varieties. At one time the area around 14th Street was one of the city's most fashionable sections —at first residential and then later, as in the usual order of things, the entertainment and shopping center of Manhattan. Delmonico's at one time ruled the restaurant world from here. Tony Pastor discovered and starred the ravishing Lillian Russell in his variety theater on 14th Street. Fashionable Tiffany's and Brentano's faced Union Square. The "Ladies' Mile" from Eighth to 23rd Street along Broadway was lined with the elegant Italian palaces that dispensed high fashion to the ladies of high fashion —A. T. Stewart & Co., James McCreery & Co., Lord & Taylor and innumerable smaller but equally chic (and expensive) shops.

Sixth Avenue north of 14th Street, on the other hand, was the city's Sin Center —the further north, the more fashionable the sin. The area in the late 1800's came to be known as the "Tenderloin" district —a *mot juste* coined by police Inspector Alexander S. Williams who, transferred from a less lucrative beat to this profit-producing precinct, remarked that for some time he had been having chuck steak but that now he was going to get "some of the tenderloin."

Today, a number of bargain stores still face 14th Street, but the center of vice (as with everything else) has moved northward (and undercover). Very little remains —not even sin— to recommend the area.

Down by the East River, extending from 14th Street to 23rd Street, sprawl Peter Cooper Village and Stuyvesant Town, two of New York City's earliest, low-income housing developments, both built and operated by the

Metropolitan Life Insurance Co. These developments, which replaced the notorious gashouse district, served as models for the others that currently line the river and have done much to alleviate the squalor that reigned supreme along the east side.

East of Peter Cooper Village is New York's new marina and seaplane base. Marginal Street, starting from the northeast corner of Stuyvesant Town, edges its way along the East River as far as the United Nations and gives you the chance for a pleasant walk or drive.

Union Square

At the meeting of Fourth Avenue, 14th Street and University Place, bounded on the north by 17th Street, lies Union Square once the Right Address for the Right Hotels, until recently Tammany Hall headquarters, traditionally the stamping (and shouting) grounds of New York City's "radicals" and organized labor.

Time, alas, has done unpleasant things to that once pleasant square. Today it is dismal and the buildings surrounding it are dirty and dingy. At one end of the Square, George Washington sits on horseback (more or less on the spot where he was joyously greeted by New York City's rejoicing citizens the day of the British evacuation of Manhattan). At the other end stands Lafayette (the work of Bartholdi who did the monumental Statue of Liberty), placed there by French-descended New Yorkers.

Even the excitement of radicalism is gone from Union Square, blunted no doubt by the lead of prosperity. Nonetheless, for some of the old glow, take a walk through the park at night. You'll hear none of the rabid speeches that fired the air in the days of Sacco and Vanzetti, but there are still some would-be John the Baptists and unacknowledged World Leaders who climb on soapboxes for their after dinner speech and have a try at changing the world.

Even the ghosts of the gaudy, baudy Gay Nineties have fled, too depressed by what's become of this once stylish part of town. A few spots here and there, though, still recall the glorious days when Mrs. Astor ruled the Four Hundred with an aristocratically elegant but mailed fist. One block east and parallel to Union Square lies Irving Place which retains some of its original charm. Washington Irving is supposed to have lived here for a spell in the red brick house on the corner of 17th street.

Gramercy Park

At the northern end of Irving Place lies unchanging Gramercy Park, one of New York's enchanted spots, a residential area done in Neo-Greek style and centered around a private park reserved for its residents. Only those with homes facing the park have a key to open its lacy iron gates. Gramercy Park, planned about 1841, was —and still is, though to a lesser degree— one of the most exclusive addresses in town. Samuel J. Tilden, Mrs. Stuyvesant Fish, Stanford White, Edwin Booth once all lived at the Park. A statue of Booth, in fact, stands in its center, a reminder that he founded the Players' Club in 1888 while living at No. 16. Today the Club has its headquarters there. Another club also started its active life at Gramercy Park —the Knickerbocker Club, New York City's first baseball club used to play in the park.

Theodore Roosevelt Memorial Home

West, at 28 East 20th Street near Fifth Avenue, easily identified by the large flag waving at its front, stands Theodore Roosevelt's birthplace and boyhood home. The house is preserved the way it was in those days and, next door, a museum houses a host of T.R. memorabilia. Both house and museum are open weekdays (except holidays) from 9 a.m. to 4:30 p.m. Admission 25c.

Madison Square

Walking north on Fifth Avenue you'll come upon its intersection with Broadway and 23rd Street. Immediately to the east lies Madison Square bordered on the east by Madison Avenue (which is born at this point) and on the north by 26th Street. Here on the northeast corner once stood Madison Square Garden, a fashionable amphitheater designed by Stanford White. The building's chief attraction, though, graced the tower top of the Garden — a superb sculpture of a nude Diana by Augustus Saint-Gaudens which in 1890 raised scores of eyebrows and voices in protest. This Madison Square Garden was razed in the 1920's and another "Madison Square Garden" erected at 50th Street and Eighth Avenue where it is neither near Madison, a square nor a garden. Diana was salvaged from the original Garden and sent to the Pennsylvania Museum of Fine Arts in Philadelphia —but only after she had become a source of civic pride and one of New York City's most attractive tourist attractions.

Stanford White didn't fare as well as Diana. He tried to satisfy both his esthetic taste for architecture and the female form by maintaining a tower studio at the Garden where he was wont to entertain his current lady friends. Poetically, it was on the Madison Square Garden roof that jealous Henry Kendall Thaw shot him.

In Madison Square you'll also find one of New York City's most curious statues. Presumably it is the statue of Lincoln's Secretary of State William H. Seward —at least, that is the inscription that it bears. Actually, it is a statue of Lincoln's body topped by Seward's head

—a somewhat odd blend since Seward was rather short and squat and Lincoln long and lean. Furthermore, Lincoln-Seward holds the Emancipation Proclamation in his hand. The reason for this strange Lincoln-Seward combination is neither symbolic nor political. The committee raising the money for a statue of Seward couldn't quite raise the entire $25,000 needed and so, as an economy measure, it accepted a cut-rate, already cast body of Lincoln that had been lying about.

Southwest of Madison Square, in the triangle formed by the intersection of Fifth Avenue, Broadway and 23rd Street, stubbornly stands the Flatiron Building contrary to the predictions of the sidewalk superintendents who saw the remarkable structure going up in 1902 and ominously warned it wouldn't stay up. The building was named the Fuller Building in honor of its daring designer —with its 21 stories, it was New York City's real skyscraper— but its shape eventually won out over Mr. Fuller and now it is officially labelled the Flatiron Building on its façade.

Church of the Transfiguration

Continuing on to the corner of Fifth Avenue and 29th, you'll find the unobtrusive Church of the Transfiguration much more widely known as the "Little Church around the Corner." The story goes that when the pastor of a fashionable church refused to conduct funeral services for a defunct actor —acting was not a profession as yet acceptable to High Society— he suggested to the deceased's friends that they try "the little church around the corner." The pastor's name has long since been forgotten but the Little Church around the Corner became famous almost overnight especially among actors. Today the Little Church around the Corner is the most popular church in the city —for weddings, not funerals.

Bellevue and NYU Medical Center

Across town by the East River, beginning at 23rd Street and ending at 34th, is one of the greatest concentrations of medical buildings in the country. On the southern end at 408 First Avenue stands the new Veterans Administration Hospital with its 1283 beds and liberal visiting hours (from 3 to 8 p.m. daily). Immediately north and extending to 30th is the impressive but ugly group of buildings comprising Bellevue Hospital. Contrary to what most people believe, this is not a psychiatric hospital —though New York City could certainly use one that size— but one of the greatest and certainly the oldest general hospital not only in the country but in North America. Of its 2684 beds only 638 are in its psychiatric wing. Above Bellevue and extending to 34th Street are the shining new buildings of the New York University Medical Center including its School of Medicine and its famed Institute of Physical Medicine and Rehabilitation.

On the west part of town, between 23rd Street and 29th Street and bounded by 9th and 10th Avenues, spreads the Penn Station South Housing Development, a group of ten 21-story apartment houses for middle income families. The development is remarkable in that it is financed and sponsored by the International Ladies' Garment Workers Union who also sponsored the co-operative Corlears Hook Houses overlooking the East River.

A historical note: not far from these modern apartment buildings, at the corner of 22nd Street and 8th Avenue, is the Stephen Merritt Burial & Cremation Company. They are the ones who conducted General Grant's funeral back in August of 1885, and the 38-star flag, framed and hanging in their office, was draped over General Grant's coffin for the funeral.

The skyscrapers of midtown Manhattan on the East Side
are topped by the spire of the Chrysler Building at right

6 | *East Side...*
| *Elegant and Elite*

Section   From 32nd Street to 59th Street, East Side.

Map   See page 127.

**First   BMT to 34th Street (Sixth Avenue) — express stop;
stop**   IND-Sixth Avenue to 34th Street — express stop; IRT-
              Lexington to 33rd Street (Park Avenue)— local stop.

**Where   Al Schacht's, Brasserie, Café Chambord, Café Louis
to eat**   XIV, Danny's Hide-A-Way, Exchange Restaurant,
              Four Seasons, Gripsholm, Hapsburg House, Harvey's,
              Janssen's, Le Marmiton, Le Pavillon, Luau 400, Old
              Brew House, Pen & Pencil, P. J. Moriarty's, Polonaise,
              Quo Vadis, Sardi's East, Swiss Pavilion, Top of the
              Six's, Trader Vic's.

**Sights   Empire State Building, New York Public Library,
for the   United Nations, Union Carbide Atomic Energy Ex-
children**   hibit, Pepsi Cola gallery, IBM Arts & Science Gallery.

By the 1870's, High Society had abandoned Greenwich Village —had even abandoned Lower Fifth Avenue. It clustered now, in rows of opulent brownstone and marble mansions, along the short stretch between 34th and 42nd Streets on Fifth, Madison and Park Avenues —the Murray Hill area, New Yorkers' equivalent of the Valley of the Kings. Here Astor & Sons built their various Italian *palazzi*. The upstart, A. T. Stewart —a mere tradesman, though High Society flocked to his fashionable department store— dared to have his even more magnificent palace on the northwest corner of 34th and Fifth. Across the way, *the* Mrs. William Astor looked upon him with disdain. John Pierpont Morgan had erected his monumental mansion at Madison and 37th.

A century earlier a different aristocracy had ruled the Hill. Quakers Robert and Mary Murray had entertained British nobility. One September 15th in 1776, Mary Murray with irresistible hospitality had persuaded British General Howe to dally a while over a cup of tea. While Howe sipped, American Revolutionary General Putnam —and his army— slipped through British fingers and rejoined an anxious General Washington.

Time has changed Murray Hill: the hill has been leveled and the Valley of the Kings has new rulers. Tall, sleek luxury hotels, apartment houses and office buildings of glass and steel have replaced the brownstone and marble. Fifth Avenue, once the citadel of the aristocratic and the wealthy, is now the bastion of the glamorous women's shops, chic specialty stores, and elegant hotels. B. Altman, W. J. Sloan, Lord & Taylor, I. Miller, Rogers Peet, Finchley, Peck & Peck, Black Starr & Frost, Saks Fifth Avenue, Best & Co., De Pinna, Cartier, Georg Jensen, the Hotels Gotham and St. Regis, Bonwit Teller, Tiffany's, Tailored Woman, Bergdorf Goodman, F. A. O. Schwarz, Plummer's, the Plaza Hotel and Hotel Savoy Hilton, etc. stretch out in a glittering row to the green borders of Central Park. Ruling over all those on Fifth Avenue from its corner on 34th Street is the giant among giants —the beautiful, soaring Empire State Building.

Empire State Building

Without much question, next to the Statue of Liberty, the Empire State Building is New York City's most well known tourist attraction. It first started reaching for the stars at a time when man's hopes were at their lowest ebb. Incredibly, plans for its construction were announced on August 30th, 1929 and, despite Black Friday, work was started on March 17th, 1930. In May 1931, with its

The Empire State Building at night
outshines Manhattan's other lights
(top). The Empire State Building
(right) against a dusky sky.

head 1250 feet into the clouds, it was opened to the
public.

Life hasn't been too easy for this king of buildings.
Many things have happened to it that would have cowed
another less noble edifice. It has been struck by lightning
innumerable times. It was even struck by aircraft one
foggy night. (Today its four powerful beams —the "Freedom Lights"— make it the tallest lighthouse in the world,
visible for 300 miles.) Worst blow of all, it was struck
by its elevator operators a decade or so ago and almost
crippled. (Some automatic elevators have since been in-
stalled.) In 1950 the Empire State Building was topped by a
22-story, 60-ton television tower sending another 222
feet into the clouds. But in 1954 it lost its title of the
world's tallest structure when a 1572-foot TV antenna
went up outside Oklahoma City, Okla. —this monster

has since been superseded by at least four other antenna towers— and in 1970 the Building King is scheduled to lose its title of world's tallest building to the twin towers of the World Trade Center.

Nonetheless, the Empire State Building remains a wondrous thing to behold, and the view from its 102nd story observatory will always be breathtaking. On a clear day, visibility is 80 miles and you will be able to see, stretching out around you, Massachusetts, Connecticut, Pennsylvania, New Jersey and New York. Seeing the teeming army of ants scurrying back and forth 1250 feet below will have a very sobering effect —you'll suddenly be struck by the thought of how infinitely small you must appear to the Creator. At night the view is perhaps even more spectacular for New York City is at its sparkling, jewel-like best.

The Empire State Building is open every day from 9:30 a.m. to midnight except on Christmas Eve. Admission to one or both observatories (on the 86th and 102nd stories) is $1.50 for adults, 75c for children under 12.

J. P. Morgan Library

Two blocks north and one east of the Empire State Building, at the corner of Madison Avenue and 36th Street, stands the magnificent J. P. Morgan Library which the fabulous financier had built for himself in 1906 and which he spent fortunes (sacking Europe of its art treasures) to fill. He applied the same relentless determination to amass these art treasures as he had applied to amassing the greenbacks —and trusts. In an era when all millionaires were art collectors (not so much by taste as by the desire to keep up with the aristocratic Joneses), J. P. Morgan outstripped them all.

You will see some of the results of J. P.'s insatiable

acquisitiveness at the John Pierpont Morgan Library which his son in 1924 turned over to the public —thus fulfilling a wish expressed in his father's will. It holds one of the most valuable collections of rare books, beautiful illuminated manuscripts, prints, etc. (though not all are on exhibit to the public simultaneously). Among the library's prizes is the *Constance Missal* (one of three extant copies) which many scholars believe Gutenberg printed from type about 1450 —some seven years before printing the Gutenberg Bible. The Missal was valued at more than $100,000 at the time it was purchased from the Capuchin monks in Romont, Switzerland back in 1954.

The library is open weekdays and Saturdays from 9:30 a.m. to 5:00 p.m. It is closed all Sundays and holidays, and Saturdays during the months of June, July and August. Admission is free.

Incidentally, directly across town at Second Avenue is the entrance to the Queens Midtown Tunnel (opened to traffic in 1940). Neighboring it (at 37th and First Avenue) is the modern East Side Airlines Terminal with airline coaches going to and from La Guardia and Kennedy Airports. Neither the tunnel nor the terminal are worth making a trip to see, but you may want to use them some day. Toll for the tunnel is 25c for passenger cars. Fee for the airline coach service is $1.50 per person.

New York Public Library

Return to Fifth Avenue and walk north along this famous street to 41st Street. (You'll want to window shop along the way —unless both your wallet and your resistance are low.) Between 41st and 42nd Streets, on the west side of Fifth Avenue, stop in reverence before that wonderful institution —the New York Public Library, or rather, the Central Research Branch of the New York

'Patience' looks down on Fifth Avenue from its pedestal on the steps of the N.Y. Public Library

Public Library which, together with the 80 Circulating Branches, make up the largest public library system in the world. With 3 million or so visits paid to it annually and with 4 million volumes for its visitors to thumb, it is also reputedly the most used library in the western world.

The building itself is noteworthy: a neo-classic palace of almost overpowering dignity, started in 1902 and completed in 1911 on the site where once stood the Croton Reservoir, a favorite excursion spot for New Yorkers during the last half of the 19th century. On either side of the somewhat worn marble steps leading to the main entrance, a lion sits looking with leonine disdain upon the Fifth Avenue traffic. The felines —Mayor La Guardia once nicknamed them "Patience" and "Fortitude"— are almost as famous as the library itself which occasionally receives mail addressed to "The Lion Library."

The Central Research Branch isn't just meant for the student, the scholar and the writer. Its magnificent building (both the interior and exterior) and the special exhibits on display throughout its three floors are worth seeing even if you are at best only a casual reader. Of special interest: an exhibit on the development of printing; the U. S. Postage Stamp collection; manuscripts and rare editions of Washington Irving, its first president; exhibits of paintings, prints, etc. from its collection.

Behind the library, occupying what was once a potter's field, lies Bryant (for William Cullen Bryant) Park, a small formal affair liberally sprinkled with park benches. The park is on Sixth Avenue and belongs, thus, on the west side. It is mentioned in this east side ramble because one of the Fifth Avenue library's best loved public services is the broadcasting of recorded concerts in Bryant Park, between noon and 2 p.m., for the benefit of the midtown office workers—and millions of pigeons—who enjoy having their sandwich lunch in the park on fine summer days while listening to good music. Also enjoying the music, at the Sixth Avenue and 42nd Street corner of the park, is the bronze statue of the Brazilian hero, José Andrade, donated by Brazil.

At 42nd Street turn east and walk two blocks down to Pershing Square (underneath the Park Avenue ramp). Here stands the Official Visitors' Information Center of the New York Convention and Visitors Bureau, your friend in need and in deed. The Bureau will (or does its best to) answer the million and one questions New York City's 14 million annual visitors ask plus provides free descriptive literature on New York City's sights, hotels, restaurants, shops, events, etc.

Grand Central Terminal

Directly across the way from Pershing Square, blocking Park Avenue and extending east to Lexington Avenue, is that product of Vanderbilt shrewdness —the mammoth Grand Central Terminal. When Vanderbilt first opened his station to the public (1913), it certainly was grand (it took ten years to finish) but it was hardly central. Some people had already jumped the Harlem River but most New Yorkers were concentrated in the area below 42nd Street. Nonetheless, more than 80 trains arrived and departed daily at the new station.

Today Grand Central Terminal is still not in the center of New York City —and not even of Manhattan— but more than 550 trains arrive and depart daily on the 123 tracks on its two levels. Principal attraction of the terminal is the huge and spacious main concourse. More people pass through it yearly (including those just passing by) than the total population of the United States. Most of them rush by hardly stopping to glance at the exhibits in the great hall —among them the latest automobile models and the world's largest color photo— or the many shops along the concourse, but even a small percentage of that great multitude is enough to keep the shops flourishing and the exhibits worth their keep.

Incidentally, at the Terminal's lower level, underneath the arches in front of the Oyster Bar, an accoustical phenomenon permits you to carry on a whispered conversation with anyone in the corner diagonally across the way from you. For it to work, however, you must stand facing your corner with lips close to the arch. Onlookers may decide you're a likely candidate for a strait jacket but they are accustomed to these oddities. At one time or another every New Yorker starts talking to himself.

Pan Am and Chrysler Buildings

Looking down impassively on Grand Central Terminal and the people that scurry in and out of its numerous entrances is the octagonal Pan Am Building which is billed as the *largest* office building in the world and regurgitates some 25,000 people at the end of a working day (many of whom, no doubt, add to the general commotion at Grand Central Terminal during the rush hours). The Pan Am Building sports a heliport as a roof top from where you may take a helicopter to any one of the airports servicing New York City —or on a bird's eye tour of the city, if you wish.

Continuing east along 42nd Street, on the northeast corner of Lexington Avenue, towers the Chrysler Building which even in this day of new skyscrapers still holds the title of the second tallest building in the world. It stands 77 stories high and 1048 feet tall in its stocking feet —if you take into consideration its silver spire, patterned after the radiator caps that graced the Chrysler automobile models in 1929 (the year before the building was completed).

Diagonally across the corner from the Chrysler is the Chanin Building, another of the city's early (1929) skyscrapers (56 stories). Directly east of it stands a fairly recent addition to the New York City sky scene —the 45-story Socony Mobile Building. It is most notable for its self-washing, embossed steel exterior —and because beneath its modern façade it hides part of a six-story structure standing at that spot for more than half a century. It seems the Transit Authority has easement rights under the new building because they have had escalators and escalator machinery there since 1907. The best solution the constructors could find was to encase the works in the new structure.

Daily News Building

At 220 East 42nd Street, between Second and Third Avenues, stands the striking Daily News Building. The original building has been there since 1930 but the new annex, completed in 1960, makes it a product of New York City's present building boom. Star attraction of the building is in the lobby —a huge (two-ton) illuminated globe of the world revolving under a "sky canopy" of shimmering black glass rising four stories high. On the walls surrounding the globe, you'll find exhibits on the weather —including a weather dial, electrically controlled from the *News* Weather Tower on the roof, to tell you whether you should have brought your umbrella or not. Along the Second Avenue corridor are displayed enlargements of outstanding *News* photos, many of them prize-winners.

One block east of the Daily News Building between First and Second Avenues, you'll come upon Tudor City extending from 41st to 43rd Streets, once a group of very swank apartment houses designed in the Old English style with inner courts and gardens and still a "preferred" address today. Camera fans will find the bridge joining the two elements of Tudor City split by 42nd Street a vantage point for taking photos of the UN buildings directly east.

The United Nations

One of New York City's prime attractions, drawing more than 2½ million visitors yearly, does not properly belong to the city nor, for that matter, to the United States. It is the 18 international acres between 42nd and 48th Streets, fronting the East River and extending to First Avenue, and encompassing that modern Tower of Babel on which rest the hopes of many people —the

The beautiful Secretariat Building at United Nations Headquarters

United Nations Headquarters. In the opinion of many (including the writer) this group of buildings constitutes the most striking and beautiful archtectural showcase in New York City. It has served as the inspiration for many buildings that have followed —though few have approached the mark.

Some traditionalists consider the UN group a monstrosity but all will agree that, whatever else, United Nations Headquarters is a vast improvement over what had been there —one of the most blighted areas of New York City. It had not always been so. As early as 1639, the area had been the plantation known as Turtle Bay Farm of two English tobacco growers —Turtle Bay being the indentation of shoreline between 46th and 48th Streets long since filled in. Almost a century and a half later it was the scene of several skirmishes during the early part of the American Revolution and, according to tradition, Nathan Hale was hanged in 1776 from the bough of an apple tree that once stood somewhere near the corner of First Avenue and 46th Street. As New York stretched its bounds, the area became a well-to-do residential section and then finally deteriorated into a commercial section of malodorous slaughter and packing houses and crumbling tenements.

When the United Nations Site Committee began looking for a site for the UN's permanent headquarters, crowded Manhattan was purposely overlooked. Then two shrewd businessmen stepped into the picture. Real estate operator William Zeckendorf proposed to John D. Rockefeller, Jr. (one of New York City's wealthiest landlords) that regeneration of the Turtle Bay area would raise the real estate values of the surrounding area. Rockefeller thought the line of reasoning sound and promptly offered the United Nations $8½ million to purchase the site. New York City offered other inducements, among them waterfront rights and a $30 million improvement program which included widening of the adjacent streets, landscaping and an ornamental fence encircling the site's boundaries. The United Nations accepted the generous offer and, as Zeckendorf had predicted, real estate values soared. New office buildings and apartment houses sprang up like grass after a summer rain. Today "Turtle Bay" is one of Manhattan's most attractive areas. Contributing not a little to the overall beauty is the fact that of the 18 international acres only 25% are occupied by the four buildings of the United Nations. The remaining acreage is covered with gardens, trees, shrubs, fountains, plazas.

■ General Assembly Building

Entrance to United Nations Headquarters is at the level of 45th Street at the northern end of the General Assembly Building, a low, sloping structure of English limestone topped by a shallow dome. Glass panels set into marble piers form the north face of the building and produce a soft lighting effect in the 75-foot high lobby. A huge glass window — 53½ feet high— framed in marble makes up the south face. The General Assembly meets in the large auditorium in the delegates' area precisely beneath the dome of the building while visitors may watch the proceedings from the public galleries.

■ Conference Building

Behind the General Assembly Building and connecting it to the Secretariat Building is the long, low Conference Building extending 400 feet along the waterfront. The building, housing chambers and facilities for the Economic and Social, Trusteeship and Security Councils, is cantilevered over the Franklin Delano Drive. Its top floor, set back on a tiled roof, holds the delegates' dining room (which is also opened to the public), private dining rooms, a cafeteria and kitchen. Teak railing from Burma —more than half a mile of it— runs along an outside terrace on the building's lower three levels.

■ The Secretariat Building

Most of the controversy over the United Nations Buildings' architectural merits (or lack of them) rose over the Secretariat Building, the first to be completed. None-theless, it is also the one most imitated and, with its severely simple lines, the most striking of the group. The building stands 39 stories (505 feet) high but is only a slim 72 feet wide. Its north and south faces, 289 feet long, consist entirely of aluminum and blue-green glass windows (specially treated to reduce glare and absorb the heat from the sun's rays). The slender east and west sides are of solid gray Vermont marble —2,000 tons of it.

A staff of 3500 men and women from 100 or so countries work in the Secretariat Building and 4000 in-dividual air conditioning controls (with a 12° temperature variation range) help them keep cool —at least, climatic-ally speaking. The building faces a plaza with a fountain and circular reflecting pool —a gift to the United Nations from the children of the United States and its territories. The black pebbles used to form the black serpentine lines in the floor of the pool were collected and contributed by Greek women and children from the Island of Rhodes.

- **Dag Hammarskjold Library**

The most recent addition to the United Nations group, standing at the southwest corner of the site, is the Dag Hammarskjold Library, dedicated on November 16th, 1961 in honor of the late Secretary-General to the UN. The six-story building —three above and three below ground— has a two story reading room, an auditorium and room enough to accommodate 400,000 volumes.

- **Facilities for Visitors**

The United Nations buildings are open daily in-cluding holidays from 9:00 a.m. to 6:00 p.m. (The Book Shop, Gift Centre, Souvenir Shop and Stamp Sales Coun-ter, however, are closed on Christmas and New Year's.) You may check your coat in the cloakroom on the Public

Concourse free of charge. Cameras are permitted and you will be told in what area you may take pictures. (No tripods are allowed, though.) If you are female and 13 years or over, you must wear a dress or a skirt. No slacks or shorts are permitted on the United Nations premises.

Near the Headquarters' entrance at the General Assembly Building, a circular information desk is staffed with multi-lingual personnel ready to answer your questions on the UN. Nearby a limited number of free tickets to the General Assembly meetings are distributed on a first come, first served basis. (Individual seats cannot be reserved in advance since the meeting schedules tend sometimes to be erratic.)

Guided tours of the United Nations Headquarters start at the south (or opposite) end of the building and leave about every few minutes between 9 a.m. and 4:45 p.m. The tours last approximately an hour and cost $1.00 for adults. Students and children, however, may take the tour at half price, while service men and clergy are treated even better —for them the tour is free. Children under five are not permitted on a tour.

Free United Nations motion pictures are shown from 10:30 a.m. to 4 p.m. whenever a conference room is available for the showing.

The Delegates' Dining Room is open Mondays through Fridays and you may have lunch there but you will only be seated before 11:45 a.m. or after 2 p.m. as seats become available. If you're male, you *must* wear a jacket. Cost of lunch ranges from $2.00 to $3.25.

Park Avenue

Your next destination lies up a pace from the United Nations through Hammarskjold Plaza to the corner of 47th Street and Park Avenue. But first a word

about this famous boulevard. Not too long ago Park
Avenue was lined with intimidating apartment buildings,
the last word in elegance and chic. If you had an address
on Park Avenue, you were a member of café society, a
frequenter of the 21 Club, the Stork Club, El Morocco,
etc. During the last decade or so Park Avenue has been
transformed. It remains the ultimate in elegance and its
inhabitants still frequent the 21 Club, the Stork Club,
etc. —but on company expense accounts. The chic addresses now belong to the café society of companies and
corporations for Park Avenue has become a showcase of
sleek, modern office buildings.

Union Carbide Building

A gleaming glass and steel example stands at the
corner of 47th Street: No. 270 Park Avenue, the 52-
story Union Carbide Building, one of the tallest on Park
Avenue and one of the most arresting. It has other things
to interest you, however, besides its modern design. On
its second floor a block-long "Atomic Energy in Action"
exhibit (one of the best of its kind) graphically explains
all —or, at least enough for the layman—about atomic
energy and how it is being put to peaceful uses. Included
in the exhibit is the world's largest model of an uranium
atom. Highlight, though, is a full-scale operating model
of an atomic research reactor with a running narration
synchronized with each of the reactor's operating phases.

Just north of the Union Carbide Building is the
smaller Bankers Trust building, another jewel of an edifice. Immediately following it are the modern Colgate-
Palmolive Building and the architectural twins, the ITT
and the Manufacturers Hanover Bank Buildings.

Across the way from the Union Carbide Building,

on the east side of Park Avenue, stands the block-filling Chemical Bank New York Trust Company. This is followed by the elegant Park Lane Hotel and the even more elegant, immense and famous Waldof Astoria, usually the New York home of visiting royalty and nobility. Occupying the entire width of the block between 50th and 51st Street is the fashionable (and comparatively new) St. Bartholomew's Episcopal Church, built in the Byzantine style. It has one of the largest episcopal congregations in the country and is the scene of many socialite weddings.

St. Patrick's Cathedral

Directly west on 51st Street between Madison and Fifth Avenues, stands St. Patrick's Cathedral. Its main entrance, however, is on Fifth Avenue.) St. Patrick's was designed by James Renwick (architect of the Grace Church downtown) and is considered about the finest example of the neo-Gothic to be found in the United States. When it was first started in 1858, this part of Fifth Avenue was still regarded as "the country." However, by the time it was consecrated in 1910 St. Patrick's was pretty much in the center of things.

Today the Cathedral is hemmed in on almost all sides by towering office buildings (most notably, the Rockefeller Center group), so that it is impossible to find a completely unobstructed view of the entire edifice. Nonetheless, the Cathedral is especially noted for its beautiful exterior and interior detail and the office buildings won't interfere with your admiration of these.

Before entering, note particularly the lacy rose window over the entrance as well as the handsome bronze doors with their intricate carved detail and statues set in niches. Inside the Cathedral you'll be struck by the fine

Top view of St.
Patrick's Cathedral
and the door of its
main entrance.

marble pulpit and central altar and the outstanding
stained glass windows —there are 70 of them. In the
afternoon, the sun streaming through the rose window
makes it particularly lovely. Of the 17 side chapels, that
of Our Lady is the most outstanding and, incidentally,
the setting for many Catholic weddings.

After your inspection of St. Patrick's Cathedral
return to Park. Turn left and continue your northward
stroll along this glittering avenue. One building will stand
out among the rest —because it is so different: the famed
and venerable Racquet & Tennis Club between 52nd and
53rd Street, still elegant, still plush though it was built in
1918 in the Italian renaissance manner.

Directly opposite the club stands the imposing
Seagram Building, a striking combination of bronze and
tinted glass rising 38 stories high. A large plaza lined with

pools and giant gingko trees on either side sets the building apart and contributes to making it one of New York
City's most outstanding. Rumor has it that the upkeep
on the building is enormous —cleaning the bronze panels
is a difficult job— but possibly the fact that the building
is considered an architectural masterpiece does much to
assuage the pain the owners must feel in the region of
the wallet. Tours are conducted through parts of the
Seagram Building Tuesdays and Thursdays at 3 p.m. by
appointment only.

Directly north of the Seagram Building stands
another block-filling monument to glass and steel —the
First National City Bank Building occupying the block
between 53rd and 54th Streets. Across the way, on the
west side of Park Avenue, is the beautiful, cantilevered
Lever House with its spacious plaza —something of an
architectural landmark for it was the first building in New
York City to make use of those new-fangled glass walls.

Completely across town (but not worth a special
trip), on the East River between 54th and 59th Streets,
stretches smart Sutton Place. The chic apartments overlooking the river used to be rundown tenements until
about the 1920's when Mrs. William K. Vanderbilt decided the view was too good to waste on slums and
made that part of town fashionable. Neighboring smart
Sutton is the toll-free Queensboro Bridge, a rather ugly
(but extremely functional) product of the early 1900's
—98,000 people use it on an average day.

Continue along Park Avenue to 57th Street, one
of New York City's widest crosstown thoroughfares and
one of its most elite shopping districts. Besides some very
swank women's stores (Henri Bendel's, Jay Thorpe, etc.),
you'll find shops specializing in home furnishings and an-
tiques and some of the finer art galleries in the city.

At the 57th Street between Park and Madison Avenues is a unique museum which few New Yorkers get to see; which, in fact, most New Yorkers don't even know exists: the Scalamandré Museum of Textiles with a permanent exhibit of the textiles used in the restoration of historic homes and sites throughout the country (including the White House). The museum is open to the public every weekday (except major holidays) from 9 a.m. to 5 p.m., admission free.

Further along, on the southwest corner of Madison and 57th Street, the IBM Corporation's World Headquarters offers hour-long tours of its Products Display Center (at 10 a.m. and 3 p.m.) which include explanations and demonstrations of its computers and other business machines. The exhibit hall, itself, is opened to the public from 9 a.m. to 5 p.m. Around the corner at 16 East 57th Street, IBM also has its Arts and Science Gallery with free exhibits (changed monthly) of art, prints, photographs, etc. The gallery is open weekdays from 9:30 a.m. to 5 p.m.; Saturdays from 11 a.m. to 5 p.m.

Pepsi Cola Building

North of IBM Headquarters at 500 Park Avenue stands the comparatively small —nine stories— Pepsi Cola World Headquarters, a charming building of glass and aluminum made even more charming by its policy of showing only cultural and educational exhibits —*completely non-commercial*— in its exhibition gallery.

Among those scheduled for the future are one on "Women in Politics," avantgarde paintings from Argentina, "Phenomenal Philately," "Advances in Rehabilitation," "Racing Cars," etc. The exhibits at the Pepsi Cola Exhibition Gallery are generally shown for a month (sometimes two) before they are replaced by another.

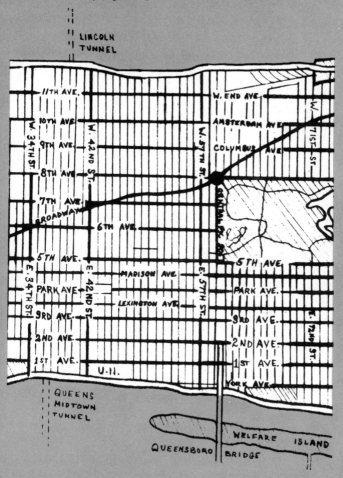

The 'gay bright way' —Rockefeller Center at Christmastime

Section	From 32nd Street to 59th Street, West Side.
Map	See page 127.
First stop	IRT-Broadway, Seventh Avenue to Penn Station (34th Street) — express stop; BMT to 34th Street (Fifth Avenue) — express stop; IND-Sixth Avenue to 34th Street (express stop).
Where to eat	The Cottage, Davy Jones, Fornos, Forum of the XII Caesars, Golden Horn, Gransons, Holland House Taverne, House of Chan, Karachi, Keen's English Chophouse, La Fonda del Sol, Larre's, Les Pyrenées, Liborio, Lindy's, Mamma Leone's, Mayan, Miyako's, Philippine Garden, P. J. Moriarty's, Ruby Foo's, Russian Tea Room, Sardi's West, Sea Fare, Steuben Tavern, Teheran, Toffenetti's, Toots Shor, 21 Club.
Sights for the children	Macy's Thanksgiving Day Parade, Rockefeller Center, Radio City Music Hall, Chase Manhattan Money Museum, Museum of Modern Art.

7

West Side . . . Sinful and Saucy

While the east side has ever been the stronghold of the elegant and the elite, the west side has acquired the reputation of being the gayest, liveliest, *most sinful* part of town. Wayward Broadway, that boulevard of pleasures, in its erratic westward course has given to the inelegant west side a saucy glamor —at least, by reputation— all its own. Withersoever Broadway went, thitherward followed entertainment and —as our Puritan Fathers so ominously warned us— Sin. Such a seductive combination is, of course, irresistible and everyone, naturally, wants to give his regards to Broadway.

Strangely enough, though the "Gay White Way" crosses the entire 13.4-mile length of Manhattan into the Bronx, it is only "gay" and "white" (or, rather, bright) for a little more than ten short blocks. The attributes that have given Broadway its international fame —its legitimate theaters, its restaurants and bars, its movie and "fun" houses— are roughly between 42nd and 53rd Streets and, furthermore, most are not *on* but just *off* Broadway. Sin, on the other hand, has devoted itself mostly to that garish, carnival-like street —Forty

Second— with its eternally bright neon lights, its lurid movie house marquees, its blaring phonographs and its population of panhandlers, pimps, prostitutes and purveyors of pornographic photographs. However, such is the magic of Broadway's ten short blocks that visitors come to the west side expecting to find it covered with —God knows what. Even New Yorkers turn to the west side to escape the boredom of their television sets. Yet, the garment industry, the city's most important, is concentrated on the frivolous west. So are America's greatest television and radio facilities —the National Broadcasting System in the RCA Building at Rockefeller Center and the Columbia Broadcasting System in its painfully new headquarters at Seventh Avenue between 52nd and 53rd Streets. And New Yorkers, themselves, will be surprised to learn that the west side also boasts of the world's busiest railroad station, a distinction they usually accredit to Grand Central Terminal on the east.

Greeley and Herald Squares

In short, the west side is a good many other things to a good many people, and about as good a place as any to start discovering what these things are is at Greeley Square, the little triangle formed by the intersection of Broadway and the Avenue of the Americas and bounded on the south by 32nd Street. Here sits Horace Greeley who, following his own advice, went "west" (at least, west side). He looks north to Herald Square which he was wont to overlook from his offices as *Herald Tribune* editor in the days the Herald Tribune was published on the Square. Here, incidentally, you'll find one of New York City's most famous clocks. Every hour two mechanical men hammer out the hour on a large bell by the legs of a statue of Minerva.

Macy's Thanksgiving Day Parade

Gimbel's and Macy's

West of these two squares extends New York City's most congested shopping district, a congestion mostly caused by the two rivalling giants of the trade: Gimbel Brothers (between 32nd and 33rd Streets) and R. H. Macy & Co. (the world's largest department store filling the entire block between 34th and 35th Streets and Broadway and Seventh Avenue). Sandwiched between the two titans is little Saks-34th Street, the poorer cousin of Saks-Fifth Avenue, who minds its own business selling women's clothes and accessories and ignores the feuders.

Macy's fame lies not just in being the world's largest department store but in the Macy's Thanksgiving Day Parade —a tradition almost 40 years old. This unique parade has come to rival the St. Patrick's Day Parade and the Easter Parade in the hearts of New York City's youngsters who gaze with wide, awe-filled eyes upon Macy's huge, helium-filled balloons —Popeye, Mickey Mouse, Donald Duck, a dinosaur, an astronaut, etc.— that float overhead. It takes about seven hours to fill one of these monstrous balloons and only the strongest Macy male employees are entrusted with the job of holding them during the parade. Oversize floats, bands and some 700 costumed Macy employees complete the picture. The parade starts at 77th Street and Central Park West and makes its way for a two-mile stretch to Macy's. It is almost a year in preparation — and lasts little more than an hour. Nonetheless, that hour is exciting enough for the children to remember the rest of the year.

Penn Station and the General Post Office

A block west of Gimbel's, occupying the enormous block between Seventh and Eighth Avenues, bustles all 23 acres of the Pennsylvania Railroad Terminal —which is rather a misnomer since the terminal serves the New York, New Haven and Hartford Railroad and the Leheigh Valley Railroad. The terminal, an example of conspicuous consumption in the Grand Manner, took $125 million to build back in 1910 when the zeros behind a dollar sign really signified something and the results are impressive. (Someone once compared it to a Roman bath —possibly because of the classic columns on its façade.) In any case, 700 trains arrive or leave from Pennsylvania

Station daily, carrying an average of 75 million passengers annually, and make it the busiest railroad station in the world. The Long Island Railroad also has a terminal in the lower level of the station and the shops lining this and the concourse along the upper Pennsylvania Railroad level sell everything —including spinettes.

Directly behind Pennsylvania Station, between Eighth and Ninth Avenues, New York City's General Post Office works desperately to keep from drowning under an ocean of mail. This post office is the world's largest mail distributing center with annual receipts exceeding more than one quarter of a billion dollars. And to think that the United States Post Office still operates in the red! Groups can make appointments to take a free guided tour of the operations on weekdays.

The Garment District

Concentrated round this section, in an area roughly beginning at 28th Street and extending to 41st Street, from Sixth to Ninth Avenues, is New York City's garment district —a chaos of trucks of all sizes and descriptions, cars, "push boys" (both men and boys pushing garment racks) and an incredible activity. New Yorkers have learned to avoid this section of the city like the plague. They've been rundown too often by a garment rack being pushed blindly from behind by a member of the ILGWU (International Ladies' Garment Workers Union) whose business it is to deliver the rack to its destination regardless of the obstacles. Still, it's a colorful section and if you're quick on your feet, and you don't mind a few bruised calves, frazzled nerves and hearing some truck drivers bawl each other out (or anyone handy) with a few choice words, then by all means walk about this part of town.

Metropolitan Opera House

A stroll northward along Seventh Avenue for five short blocks will bring you to the venerable Metropolitan Opera House, an exceedingly ugly brick building, the product of the rivalry between the *nouveau riche* (including the Morgans, the Vanderbilts, the Rockefellers) and the Old Guard (the Astors, the Belmonts, etc.). The Old Academy of Music held only 18 boxes (fully subscribed to) which left the nouveau riche out in the cold —or, at least, with orchestra seats. So the multi-millionaires decided to build their own opera house. Thus was born the Metropolitan with three tiers of 36 boxes each (later one tier was eliminated) plus a balcony and the top "family circle" affording a crow's nest view of the stage. The tiers became known as the "diamond horseshoe" and the "golden horseshoe" in descending order of social status —as measured by the number of figures at the end of your bank statement.

The opera house is still as ugly as ever though its interior retains much of the magnificence of the days when the Morgans, the Vanderbilts, the Rockefellers presented a glittering, solid front of diamonds —and the audiences came to watch the creatures in the boxes rather than those on stage. You will get some idea of what it must have been like then by attending one of the Metropolitan's opening nights —usually in late October or early November. The "brewery on Broadway" (as the impressario of the old Academy of Music, with a keen sense of the appropriate, once termed the rival house), however, is on the executioner's list for the Metropolitan Opera Company will move to its new quarters in the Lincoln Center on Amsterdam Avenue and 64th Street when these are completed (scheduled for late 1965).

Whatever its faults, the Metropolitan Opera Company has some of the finest voices in the world and its dynamic manager Rudolph Bing (though the conservatives question his methods) has done much to raise it out of the doldrums into which it had lately fallen by staging brilliant new productions of old favorites and adding to the company's repertoire little performed works of merit—for example, Puccini's last opera, *Turandot*.

Lincoln Tunnel

Across town, with its entrances at Tenth Avenue between 39th and 40th Streets, the Lincoln Tunnel burrows under the Hudson River to Weekhawken, New Jersey (and incidentally to the New Jersey Turnpike). A $95 million tube, opened to traffic in 1957, increased the tunnel's capacity by 50% and made it the only three-tube vehicular underwater tunnel in the world. The tunnel, which carries an average of 30 million vehicles annually, charges 50c for passenger cars.

Nearby, occupying the entire block between Eighth and Ninth Avenues, between 40th and 41st Streets, and connected to the Lincoln Tunnel by ramp, is the modern, recently expanded Port Authority Bus Terminal —also the largest of its kind in the world. More than 200,000 passengers and 7000 buses roll in and out of the tunnel daily. One block north of the Bus Terminal on West 42nd Street is the West Side Airlines Terminal providing airport coach service ($1.35 per person) to Newark Airport in New Jersey (oddly enough, about the closest airport to midtown Manhattan in driving time —20 minutes).

East of the terminal, glitters and blares 42nd Street —especially the section from Eighth to Sixth Avenue— with movie houses featuring lurid films (but even more lurid marquees), record stores pounding out the latest record craze and shops featuring souvenirs, "fire" sales and phony auctions. Beware, beware! This part of 42nd Street is not meant for the wide-eyed innocent and the gullible. Whatever you do, don't carry your camera —not openly, at any rate— unless you happen to be a confirmed New Yorker and inured to such things. With your camera in view, you'll be approached by all types —most of them unsavory.

Times Square

At the meeting of Broadway and 42nd Street, basking in the glow of thousands of neon signs, shines famed Times Square. (The *New York Times* offices have long since moved to larger quarters around the corner at 43rd Street and the Times Tower is presently being torn down but Times Square remains *the* Time Square, the scene of that annual madness which afflicts New Yorkers and visitors alike on New Year's Eve. On that day, New Yorkers who notoriously —or so people claim— are on speaking terms with no one, pound each other's backs, embrace each other, kiss each other and generally exhibit other such behavior bordering on the lunatic. Should you happen to be in town at the time, it's safer (though possibly not as much fun) to watch the mad scene on television in the security and seclusion of your hotel room.

Underneath the Tower and, in fact, underneath several blocks is the maze known as Times Square Station, the busiest subway station in New York City (it has over 40 million paying customers yearly) —and the most confusing. (Should you happen to get lost in Times Square Station, your best bet is to come up for air, orient yourself and try again.) A shuttle service connects this station to its almost equally busy (just under 40 million paying customers annually), equally as confusing sister, Grand Central Station, on the east side and a series of colored fluorescent bulbs are designed to lead you to the shuttle. However, by the time you've disentangled yourself, you might just as well have walked the necessary four (albeit long) blocks to the east side.

Directly north of the tower, smack in the middle of the triangle formed by the intersection of 43rd Street and Broadway, stands another friend in need —the Times Square Information Center of the Department of Commerce and Public Events which will answer all your questions on New York City —whether of a commercial, industrial or just general nature. The Center, furthermore, remains open daily from 10 a.m. to 9 p.m. except Sundays when it is open until 6 p.m.

The Theater District

From 42nd Street along Broadway to Duffy's Square at 47th Street stretches an almost solid line of Manhattan's first run, first rate movie houses. Above their bright marquees shine the even brighter lights of Broadway's "Spectaculars" —monstrous neon signs that wink, blink, change color, change pictures, change words, what-have-you and back again all in the space of a minute or so. One sign tells you the time, the temperature and the forecast for the day; another sign blows smoke rings; one once upon a time even had a waterfall which was liable to spray the passerby on a windy day. All along the side streets are grouped most of Broadway's 36 legitimate theaters (nightly ranging the gamut of emotions) and some of Manhattan's better restaurants.

In the triangle formed by the intersection of Broadway and Seventh Avenue and bounded on the north by 47th Street is Duffy Square. (Why these triangular greens are called squares in the face of such irrefutable geometric evidence to the contrary, the City Fathers once knew and now only the Good Lord knows.) In the "square" stands a statue of Rev. Francis P. Duffy, the famous Roman Catholic Chaplain of the 165th Regiment during World War I. Sharing the square with him is George M. Cohan, Broadway's "Yankee Doodle Dandy." And, such are the incongruencies of New York, directly north of the square one of New York City's largest, touristy nightclubs —the Latin Quarter— features near-naked women, lavish costumes and not much else in the way of talent. (Who needs talent, did you say?)

Madison Square Garden

By 48th Street both theaters and movie houses are starting to thin out and Broadway begins to take on a quieter tone. West of Broadway, on Eighth Avenue between 49th and 50th Streets, spreads that hulk of a building known as Madison Square Garden so called for no better reason than that it was built to replace the original smaller, elegant "Garden" on Madison Square which was razed in 1925. The similiarity between the two ends with the name. The present Madison Square Garden is an enormous indoor arena seating some 18,000 spectators and featuring anything from dog shows and circuses to concerts and revival meetings. The specialty of the house, however, is sports and the arena, in fact, is billed as the "Sports Capital of the World." Price of admission depends upon the event being presented and may vary anywhere from $1.00 to $100 and up for a ringside seat to a championship match.

By 53rd Street the movie houses and theaters have played themselves out and the Great White Way suddenly becomes a showcase for automobiles: Lincoln-Mercury, Ford, Peugeot-Renault, Buick, Triumph, Dodge, Chrysler, Plymouth, Cadillac, Chevrolet, Pontiac —showrooms line the boulevard all the way up to 58th Street.

The Weather Star

On the way, between 55th and 56th Streets, Broadway passes a building best seen from a distance: that of the Mutual Life Insurance Company of New York which is topped by a star set atop a mast. Both the mast and the star will tell you the weather 12 hours in advance —if you know how to interpret their signals. Lights flashing up the mast indicate the outlook is warmer; lights moving down the mast predict cold weather ahead. If the star on top of the mast is green, fair weather is in store for you; if the star turns orange, things are apt to look cloudy. However, if that orange star starts blinking, watch out, rain is on the way. Worse still, if the star turns white and flashes, you had best get out your snow-shoes.

So much for wayward Broadway. East of it the bright lights give way to pleasures of a more cultural sort. At 43rd Street, for example, walking east towards what most New Yorkers persist in calling Sixth Avenue (though Mayor Fiorello La Guardia changed it to Avenue of the Americas ages ago), you'll come upon Town Hall (at 113 West 43rd Street) which features anything from lectures to chamber music.

General Society of Mechanics and Tradesmen

A block north and east of Town Hall, at 20 West 44th Street stands a limestone and brick building that has been there for almost a century. The society which it houses, however —the General Society of Mechanics and Tradesmen of the City of New York— is a century older than the building. Its members, in fact, marched at the funeral of "Brother Benjamin Franklin." The Society operates a free Apprenticeship School —the oldest existing technical school in America, founded in 1820— and a library of 140,000 volumes. The Society also maintains a museum and fascinating lock collection open to the public daily from 9 a.m. to 5 p.m., free of charge. The lock collection which was donated by a member and is carried on through an endowment ranges from early Egyptian wooden locks to the up-to-date time locks.

A few blocks north is the principal diamond center in the United States —the block between Sixth and Fifth Avenues on 47th Street. Here most of New York City's diamonds are bought, cut, polished, fitted and sold. You'll find the shop windows sparkling with the end products of this activity. Most of the buildings on this street, by the way, do not have entrances going through to the next street. The dealers in diamonds feel uncomfortable in buildings that would give jewel thieves the chance to run in one end and out the other.

Rockefeller Center

Starting on the next street (48th) and covering an area extending to 52nd Street between Fifth and Sixth Avenues, spreads another of New York City's top attractions, that amazing complex of (now) 17 buildings known as Rockefeller Center.

To make way for the Center, almost 300 houses, shops and speakeasies, butting against each other in ugly rows of brownstone, were demolished. The original plan had been to build a business and entertainment center with a new opera house —to replace the architectural and acoustical monstrosity still standing at 39th and Broadway— as the focal point. The Great Depression caused a change of plans —New Yorkers faced with bankruptcy and imminent starvation were in no mood for the Finer Things in Life. The opera house idea was abandoned (for thirty years as it turned out) and John D. Rockefeller, Jr., caught with a $3 million annual rent* on his hands for the site, proceeded to do something about it. Rockefeller Center, started as a result in the wobbly 30's, has proven to be one of the most solid products of the depression.

The Center has been much publicized by its press agents as "the city within a city" —and for once the press agents were caught telling the truth. In its few blocks are concentrated 40,000 semi-permanent "residents" —the men and women who work for the tenant companies— already a fair size community by any standards. Another 160,000 come calling daily —either for pleasure or to do business— making the daytime population density of Rockefeller Plaza one of the highest in the world. In addition, a small army —880 night workers— keep the Rockefeller Center buildings clean while another army washes its 25,174 windows once a month.

The complex can also boast of two schools, 26 restaurants (serving anything from hot dogs to filet mignon à la Chateaubriand —at prices ranging from inexpensive to exorbitant), more than 200 shops and services (selling anything from bobby pins to an around-the-world luxury cruise), the world's largest indoor theater and one of New York City's most unique museums.

---

* Columbia University was then and is now the happy landlord and in 2069 —unless the lease is renegotiated— will become the owner which is probably the main reason why Columbia University Students boastfully sing: "Oh, who owns New York? Oh, who owns New York?, some people say. Why we own New York. Why, we own New York. Who? C-o-l-u-m-b-i-a!"

■ **International Section**

The best time to see Rockefeller Center is in the spring or early summer when its landscaped plazas, terraces and four acres of rooftop gardens bloom with an exuberance all the more appreciated because of the great dirth of it elsewhere in Manhattan. Start from the Fifth Avenue side for the best first look at the complex. Most of the buildings you'll see facing the Avenue are known as the International Section. However, the first building on the south (at the northwest corner of 48th Street) is the Sinclair Building recently added (by purchase) to the Rockefeller group.

The next building in line on Fifth Avenue is the small Maison Française with a sculptured panel at the entrance depicting New York and Paris joining hands over the female figures of Poetry, Beauty and Elegance (though to many observors, the naked figure of Beauty loses her title to both Poetry and Elegance).

Across from the Maison Française, separated by a landscaped walk officially called the Promenade but more commonly dubbed the "Channel Gardens," stands the architectural twin of Maison Française —the British Empire Building. In contrast to the former building, the entrance to the British Empire Building is restrained. Nine bronze figures set in the door represent the basic British industries.

Next on Fifth Avenue is the 41-story, double winged International Building with its southern wing known as the Palazzo d'Italia. In the forecourt of the building, Lee Lawrie's powerful bronze sculpture of Atlas —probably the Center's most well known work of art, certainly its most photographed one— bends under the weight of a world (composed of bronze hoops) which he carries 45 feet high.

■ Channel Gardens

To see the other buildings of the Center, walk
through the Channel Gardens leading to the sunken
Rockefeller Plaza. This is one of the few places in rush-
rush New York that even the proverbially hurried New
Yorker, suddenly afflicted by spring fever, will pause to
enjoy. Forsythia, azaleas, iris, tulips blossom along the
rectangular pools stretching the length of the Promenade
and fountains sparkle in the sun. The more unconven-
tional New Yorkers —and, of course, the visitors— go
so far as to make use of the benches lining the pools and,
in summer, watch the goldfish swishing back and forth
under the water lilies. In winter the Promenade may be
devoid of blossoms but not of imagination. For the

Atlas and the
International
Building

Christmas holidays it is transformed into a bright strip of Christmas lights and Christmas motifs. At the end of the Promenade can be seen the huge Rockefeller Plaza Christmas tree, a blazing mass of almost 4000 firefly lights and illuminated colored bulbs.

■ Prometheus and the Sunken Plaza

Beyond the promenade is Rockefeller Center's sunken plaza dominated by the twice-as-big-as life gilded bronze figure of the fire-bringer Prometheus carrying his gift to mankind. In the summer, the sunken plaza becomes an international café with gay parasol-covered tables; in the winter it is transformed into an ice skating rink. Above and surrounding it fly the flags of the United Nations and, almost inevitably, regardless of the season, an unhurried crowd looking down on the diners or the skaters or simply enjoying the sun. At Eastertime the Rockefeller Center Choristers, a group of 100 harmonious men and women, spend their day by Prometheus singing to anyone who cares to listen.

Bisecting Rockefeller Center directly behind the sunken plaza is a short, private thoroughfare extending from 48th to 51st Street known as Rockefeller Plaza.

■ The RCA Building

At 30 Rockefeller Plaza towers the 70-story RCA Building, the tallest of the Center. Before entering it you can't help but notice another of Lee Lawrie's works —a tremendously powerful sculptured figure of wisdom that seems to hover over the entrance. Once inside, your first impression will be of the building's overpowering lobby. High above on the ceiling, the Spanish artist José María Sert painted gigantic figures of the Past, Present and Future as though bridging the tall columns of the lobby. Above them a spiral of planes flies higher and still higher into the clouds. The effect is one of enormous height.

One of the murals in the lobby, depicting man's accomplishments, was also painted by Sert but came as an afterthought. It replaced an original mural painted (on commission from John D. Rockefeller, Jr.) by the Mexican artist Diego Rivera in 1939 who, with a rather wry sense of humor, painted Lenin in a most favorable light but was less than complimentary to Rockefeller, Sr. Rockefeller, Jr. banned the mural from Rockefeller Plaza and the work is presently ensconced in Mexico City's *Palacio de Bellas Artes* where, with all deference to the great Mexican artist, it looks exactly like what it is —a communist propaganda poster.

In the lobby of the RCA Building you'll also find a battery of multilingual receptionists on hand at information desks, daily from 9 a.m. to 5 p.m., ready to give you all sorts of general information on New York City's sightseeing, cultural and recreational activities.

On the 65th floor of the building, the Rainbow Room —open daily except Sundays from 4:30 p.m. to 12 p.m.— provides soft music, cocktails, dinner and a spectacular view of the city for anyone with the wherewithal to pay for them. (The music and view are free but they cannot be divorced from the cocktails and/or dinner which definitely are not.) The Observatory Roof —70 floors above street level— provides an even more spectacular view (including a unique one of St. Patrick's Cathedral below). $1.15 will get you to the Observatory Roof but for another 65c you may take a guided tour which will take you through the most important buildings of the Rockefeller Complex. Tours leave (usually at frequent intervals) from the Guided Tour Lounge in the RCA Building from 9 a.m. to 5 p.m. daily. The Observatory Roof is open daily from 9 a.m. to midnight.

▪ Chase Manhattan Money Museum

In the northwest corner of the RCA Building, with entrances at 1254 Avenue of the Americas, one of New York City's most unique museums —the Chase Manhattan Money Museum— draws some 100,000 visitors annually. The museum has a collection of 75,000 specimens of "money" (of which about 5,000 are on exhibit at one time) —including an ancient Babylonian clay tablet due bill more than 5000 years old, a stone worth 10,000 coconuts or (if the owner didn't happen to like coconuts) a wife, and a $10,000 Federal Reserve Note, all three very rare items, indeed. The museum is open free Tuesdays through Saturdays from 10 to 5 p.m.

▪ General Dynamics Building

Directly south of Rockefeller Center's sunken plaza stands the 36-story General Dynamics Building —the former Time & Life Building. In its lobby is a striking wood-carved mural —"Man and Nature"— by the great Swedish sculptor Carl Milles. Every hour for two full minutes a mechanical bird sings from his perch on a tree to a wooden man seated on a horse who obviously appears to enjoy the performance. So will you.

▪ RCA Exhibit Hall

Aligned behind (i.e., west of) the General Dynamics Building are the Eastern Airlines and the U. S. Rubber Buildings. RCA maintains an exhibit hall in the Eastern Airlines Building (at 40 west 49th Street) open free to the public from 11 a.m. to 8 p.m. In it you'll find an interesting display on the communications industry's latest electronic wonders as well as an opportunity to see yourself on color television.

▪ Radio City Music Hall

North of the RCA Building stand the 31-story American Metal Climax Building and its close neighbor,

Radio City Music Hall, the world's largest theater, seating 6200 spectators. Everything about this theater is giant size including the entertainment which features spectacular stage productions and first run films. The stage, for example, measure 144 feet across —a full city block. The contour curtain of the proscenium —a shimmering gold fabric— weighs three tons and requires almost a mile of bronze cable to raise and lower. The theater has 206 spotlights of which 36 use 150 amps and each cost more than a popularly priced car, etc.

Above all the theater is noted for the lavishness of its stage productions. As many as 425 different costumes are used for one show —Scheherazade. Star attraction, though, are the internationally famous, high-stepping, precision-perfect "Rockettes" —a troupe of 46 girls (only 36 appear on stage simultaneously —the other ten are vacationing) who dance as though they were one, going through their paces better (and much prettier by far) than a graduating class of West Point Cadets. Also well known is the Music Hall's *Corps de Ballet,* the only resident dance group in the country. One of the most breathtaking sights at Radio City is the Ballet's brilliant production of the exciting Ravel's Bolero, bursting with colors of fire-red and gold.

More than 180 million people have visited Radio City Music Hall since it first opened in 1932. An incredible number come to see the traditional Easter and Christmas shows and from the lines waiting to see these productions —often circling the block several times— you would think they were giving away $5 bills inside. Reserved seats (944 in the first mezzanine) are available but if you plan to visit the Music Hall during the Easter or Christmas seasons, you had best make reservations well in advance. Prices range from $.95 (weekdays

Radio City Rockettes

before noon)to $1.85 (Sundays after 1 p.m. till closing) for general admission; from $1.85 (weekdays before 3 p.m.) to $2.75 (Saturdays, Sundays and holidays after 7 p.m.) for reserved seats.

▪ Associated Press Building

Directly east of Radio City Music Hall is the Associated Press Building, home of the world's biggest news gathering service. Jutting out over the entrance is a remarkable stainless steel sculpture —the first of its kind.

▪ Time and Life Building

On the west side of the Avenue of the Americas, occupying the entire block front between 50th and 51st Streets, towers the last constructed (1959) member of the Rockefeller complex —the new Time and Life Building, 48 soaring stories of glass and steel set amid a spacious plaza of gray and white terrazzo with pools and fountains, one of the more pleasant newcomers to New York City's growing collection of glass boxes.

North of the Time and Life Building are: the City Squire Motor Inn, occupying the block between 51st and 52nd Streets on Seventh Avenue, billed as the largest motel in the world; and New York City's two newest and in-fashion hotels —the Americana between 52nd and 53rd on Seventh and New York Hilton at Rockefeller Center, between 53rd and 54th on the Avenue of the Americas.

Museum Row

East of the New York Hilton, on 53rd and 54th Streets betwen Fifth and Sixth Avenues, are clustered a group of museums offering from primitive to modern art. Walking east the first museum you'll come upon is the newly founded (1963) Museum of Early American Folk Arts at 49 West 53rd Street, a fascinating little museum with a charming collection of wooden sculptures, weathervanes, ship's figureheads, signs, wooden whirligigs, oil portraits and the like —all reflecting the artistic endeavors of our early forefathers. The museum is open Tuesdays through Sundays from 11 a.m. to 6 p.m. but a small admission fee (25c) is charged.

Almost next door, at 20 West 53rd Street, is the other swing of the pendulum —the Museum of Contemporary Crafts— featuring changing exhibits of ceramics, weaving and textiles, tapestries and rugs, metalwork and enamelling, woodwork, furniture, plastics, bookbindings, etc. The work shown is both by modern American and foreign craftsmen. The museum is open (admission free) daily from noon to 6 p.m.; Sundays from 2 p.m.

Museum of Modern Art

At 11 West 53rd Street, almost neighboring the Museum of Contemporary Crafts, stands New York City's "new" Museum of Modern Art which after almost six long months of absence —and a $25 million expansion and refurbishing program tripling its display space— New York's art lovers are joyfully welcoming back to the fold. Besides doubling the display space for its collection of paintings and sculptures, the museum has added three new galleries: the Edward Steichen Photography Center, the Paul J. Sachs Galleries for Drawings and Paintings and the Philip L. Goodwin Galleries for Architecture and Design permitting the museum to keep on exhibit from its great permanent collection much that heretofore had to remain in storage for want of appropriate display space.

Even if you don't quite approve of modern art, you'll probably find something to your taste in the museum. The photograph collection, for example, is magnificent —and understandable even to those of us who haven't been initiated into the mysteries of cubism or abstractionism or why a rubber hose entangled in pieces of scrap iron and yesterday's curlers constitutes art. The museum's no-other-like-it collection of film "classics" (both the early and the modern kind) will also appeal even to the most tradition-minded. Films are shown twice daily at 3 p.m. and 5:30 p.m. in the museum's newly refurbished auditorium.

One of the most universally pleasing parts of the museum is the just enlarged Abbey Aldrich Rockefeller sculpture garden where you may lunch (cafeteria style) or just relax amid shrubs, trees and part of the museum's collection of Rodins, Maillols, etc. The food may not be first rate, but on a lovely afternoon, the atmosphere is.

Beauty and . . . the beast (?) —Museum of Modern Art

The museum re-opens in mid-May and will be open daily from 11 a.m. to 6 p.m. except Thursdays when it will remain open until 9 p.m. and Sundays when it will not open until 2 p.m. Admission to the "new" museum is $1.00 for adults, 25c for children under 16.

Whitney Museum of American Art

Directly behind the Museum of Modern Art —you may get to it, in fact, through a passage way— is the Whitney Museum of American Art at 22 West 54th Street. This museum was founded by Gertrude Vanderbilt Whitney (the first one to think of converting an old stable at Washington Mews into an artist's studio), a talented but even wealthier sculptress who set about giving talented American artists the opportunity to show their stuff. The museum now owns the largest and most comprehensive collection of 20th century American art in the country if not in the world and continues the founder's policy of encouraging little known, young American artists. It is open (free) daily from 1 p.m. to 5 p.m. but closes all major holidays.

Museum of Primitive Art

Directly across the way is another newcomer to the New York cultural scene: the Museum of Primitive Art founded by Nelson A. Rockefeller in February 1957. The museum (housed in one of those brownstone houses that were the height of elegance at the turn of the century) has a collection —devoted primarily to the native arts of the pre-Columbian Americas, Africa and Oceania— ranging from bone carvings made in 20,000 B.C. to wood carvings from modern Africa; from art produced by prehistoric Tennessee mound dwellers to that of New Guinea's present-day headhunters. The museum is open Tuesdays through Sundays from 1 to 5 p.m. Admission is 50c for anyone 18 or over; 25c for those under 18.

Down the block at 106 West 55th Street are some ancient gaslight lamps and the signs "Bowery" and "Grand Street." Don't let the signs confuse you —and don't ask a New Yorker about them because no one will be more surprised than he to discover them there though he may have passed them hundreds of times. Bowery and Grand Street are, of course, on the Lower East Side. These street signs mark the headquarters of the Grand Street Boys Association, founded in 1920, when the members could still remember Grand Street as being a grand street. The club was founded for old times' sake —a means of renewing old acquaintances— and membership was at first restricted to those who could trace their ancestry to the Lower East Side. The signs in front of the club house today were those once by the Halfway House where immigrants used to stay before moving on to more permanent quarters. Today, with immigration restricted to a mere trickle, the Grand Street Boys have turned to charitable works and welcome as members anyone sharing their ideals.

New York City Center

Across the way at 131 West 55th Street stands the New York City Center, once an old masonic temple which passed into the hands of the City for non-payment of taxes. Then Mayor Fiorello La Guardia and Newbold Morris got together and decided to make the temple into a theater where New Yorkers could find good entertainment at popular prices —thus was born the New York City Center. That was a good twenty years ago. Today the Center is the home of the New York City

Opera Company, the City Center Gilbert & Sullivan Opera Company and the New York City Light Opera Company. Together they take turns in providing New Yorkers (and visitors) with a wide range of entertainment at prices starting with $1.95 (for second balcony seats) and going as high as $4.95 for the best orchestra seats. (Prices are fixed by the City which, in turn, only charges the City Center Companies the annual rent of $1.00. Occasionally the Center is used by an "outsider" —for example, S. Hurok— who may raise the admission price but who must really pay rent.) Don't let the City Center's comparatively low prices fool you —the entertainment is generally topnotch. Metropolitan Opera stars have often appeared with the New York Opera Company at the Center and, in fact, several had their start with the New York Opera Company.

The fall opera season at the Center usually starts in late September or early October and lasts approximately six weeks. (It generally does not conflict with the Metropolitan Opera Season.) This is followed by three or four weeks of Gilbert and Sullivan and then another three weeks or so of American opera presented by the New York Opera Company. Next comes the turn of the New York City Light Opera Company which in 1964 will depart from its usually short schedule and will end the season with an indefinite run of *My Fair Lady*.

Carnegie Hall

Diagonally across from the City Center but with its entrance on the corner of 57th Street and Seventh Avenue, stands the much revered Carnegie Hall. It stands there thanks to that flinty Scotsman Andrew Carnegie who donated the money necessary to build it but not the money to maintain it —a job he thought belonged to the community. It has been standing in that spot since 1891; it played host then to Paderewski in his first American concert.

Since the moment that it opened, Carnegie Hall has come to symbolize the finest in music, not only for New Yorkers but for the whole world. In its three-quarters of a century, it has undergone many metamorphoses which, incidentally, have left Carnegie Hall with the architectural improbability but indisputable fact that the seventh floor (front) is above the eighth floor (rear) and that to arrive at the seventh floor (rear) you may take the elevator at the front entrance to the *sixth* floor, cross over and walk *down* a flight. (If you're confused just think of how the construction workers must have felt.)

When plans for the new Lincoln Center were announced, it looked as though this time the death knell had rung for great old Carnegie. Several times during its career it had faced the executioner's block but some last minute event had saved it. No reprieve, however, was as dramatic or as close as the last in 1960. The Hall had even been sold at option and the New York builder picking up the option announced plans to erect a large office building on the site. It was saved from this fate worse than death by the builder's inability to raise the necessary cash for the project —and by famed violinist Isaac Stern and a group of Carnegie-dedicated citizens who somehow persuaded the City (through special state legislation) to buy the Hall and lease it to the Carnegie Hall Corporation, a non-profit organization, for the benefit of the public.

Following this last minute rescue, Carnegie was given a steam-bath and a new "wardrobe." Today, painted a glowing white and re-upholstered and re-carpeted in a velvety red, it is obviously still full of life and good music

The Gallery of Modern Art looks on at Columbus Circle

as witness the "International Festival of Visiting Orchestras" and other musical programs it sponsors. Admission to the concert hall naturally will vary depending upon the program being presented. However for a full symphonic concert (such as the International Festival) prices vary from $3.50 to $6.50 for the best orchestra seats.

Gallery of Modern Art

In solitary aloofness, on an island bounded by Columbus Circle, Broadway, 58th Street and Eighth Avenue, stands one of the city's most distinctive newcomers —the newly inaugurated Gallery of Modern Art including the Huntington Hartford Collection. The museum was erected and owes its permanent collection to the generosity of George Huntington Hartford II who, in turn, owes his money to all the millions of shoppers who buy at his A&P Supermarkets.

The ten-story, marble-faced building, completely blank except for some delicate marble grillwork framing the four exterior walls and a series of elongated arches across the top, was designed by Edward Durell Stone who also designed the rival Museum of Modern Art (before its recent expansion and face lifting). The Gallery of Modern Art, however, proposes to fill the gaps left by the latter, and will concentrate on heretofore neglected phases of 19th and 20th century art —i.e., representational paintings— so that this is one modern art museum you may enter feeling reasonably sure that you will recognize what you see at least in the permanent exhibits. These (taken from Mr. Huntington Hartford's collection) are displayed on the fourth and fifth floors and include among others two huge canvases by Salvador Dali and several sculptures by Jacob Epstein.

On the ninth floor the museum also has a small restaurant with a balcony and arcade offering Polynesian food and a magnificent view of Central Park.

The Gallery of Modern Art is open Tuesdays through Fridays from 12 noon to 8 p.m. and weekends from 12 noon to 6 p.m. It is closed on Mondays. Admission is 75c for adults and 25c for children under 12.

Central Park in winter

Section	From 59th Street to 110th Street.
Map	See page 169.
First stop	*East Side:* BMT to Fifth Avenue (60th Street) — express stop; IRT-Lexington Avenue to 59th Street — express stop. *West side:* IRT-Broadway, Seventh Avenue (local stop) or IND (express) to Columbus Circle 59th Street; BMT express to 57th Street (Fifth Ave.)
Where to eat	Brauhaus, Café Arnold, Chardas, Le Boeuf à la Mode, Penthouse Club, P. J. Moriarty's, Sea Fare, Stark's Steinberg's Dairy, Tavern on the Green; also, the cafeterias of the Metropolitan Museum of Art and the American Museum of Natural History.
Sights for the children	Central Park, Children's zoo, puppet shows; Metropolitan Museum of Art, Museum of the City of New York (its puppet shows, too), the Smith residence, New York Historical Society, American Museum of Natural History.

8

All Around the Park

When Central Park was purchased by the city in 1856, little old New York lay to its south, the park barely touching the northern fringes of the thriving metropolis. Nonetheless, though it was far from the center of town, by the time it was completed, the Ninth Avenue elevated and the Eighth Avenue surface cars could carry the city dwellers to their park in the "country." Commodore Vanderbilt's Grand Central Railroad, too, on its way to New England, made stops from 58th to 125th Streets. The Park, furthermore, was central to Manhattan Island: to its north spread the villages of Yorkville, Manhattanville, Carmansville and the prosperous, middle-class village of Harlem. William Cullen Bryant, the much respected editor of the *New York Post,* had fought long and eloquently in his editorial columns for this green oasis and when his pleadings at last were heard, he served on the first Park Board headed by another equally prominent, equally eloquent New Yorker, Washington Irving.

New Yorkers were rightly proud of their park. It was a radical innovation for those days —the first *planned* major park of an American city. Plans submitted by architects Frederick Law Olmsted and Calvert Vaux were chosen from among 30 others in the competitive bid and Olmsted was chosen to supervise the work necessary to carry out his design. It took more than seven years and $9 million to transform the 2½ mile long and half a mile wide rectangular wilderness of rocks and brush into a city park more than twice the size of London's famed Hyde Park, but Olmsted did his work so well that Central Park remains basically very much as it was when the famed landscape architect personally supervised almost every tree planted in the 840 acres of green. With Central Park under his belt, Olmsted went on to newer conquests —Prospect Park in Brooklyn and Riverside and Morningside Parks in Manhattan among others.

Central Park had its own conquests. The fact that this green oasis persists amid an island of concrete and glass and steel and the encroachments of "progress" is no small victory. It is also proof of civilized man's unexpressed yearning for a little less civilization and a little more untrammeled Nature. (Not that you can consider Central Park a true child of Nature. Hardly a tree grows in it that wasn't artfully planted in position.)

Hartford Pavilion

Several attempts, in fact, have been made to disturb the greenery in Central Park and the uproar has been prompt, prolonged, vociferous —and usually effective. The most recent agitation has been over the proposed Hartford Pavilion. In all innocence, George Huntington Hartford II (the same one to whom New Yorkers are indebted for the Gallery of Modern Art) offered the city a million dollars or so to erect a continental style café on the southeast corner of Central Park. New Yorkers could pause for a moment from their hurry-hurry and

—just like the Europeans— enjoy a cup of coffee, pastries, a light snack, the sun and the park. At least, that was the idea. The protests are still ringing in the park commissioner's ears. In fact, at this writing the matter continues under litigation. Meanwhile the Department of Parks has the Huntington Hartford offer and the Edward Durrell Stone designs for a smart café on its collective hands —and the southeast corner of the Park remains green and untouched, though originally the plans called for the café to be serving coffee by early 1964.

Nonetheless, though the Park changed very little through the years, it effected an almost immediate change on the city and the habits of its worthy citizens. Central Park became *the* fashion spot —Society went to be seen and the lesser folk to see.

In the winter, when the ball was up (indicating that the park's pond and lake were frozen), ice skating became the rage. The elite covered in furs arrived in sleighs while the inelegant arrived by the thousands in less stylish but equally effective modes of transportation. At night both the pond and the lake were brightly illuminated and as many as 20,000 came to take a spin on the ice.

In spring afternoons the Mall became the fashionable promenade for fashionable ladies, while on Wednesdays and Saturdays, band concerts (sponsored by the "railroads" —horse car lines— who found the large attendance profitable) brought New Yorkers (both the high and the lowly) to the Mall in droves.

The most fashionable hour in the park, though, was from four to five in the afternoon. Then all society —the famous and infamous alike— turned out in their best horse and carriage: broughams and landaus for the aristocratically conservative, barouches and victorias for the fashionably decorous, phaetons for the "smart set" crowded the carriage paths of the park. The sporting gentlemen, however, merely drove through the park in their curricles and sulkies on the way to Harlem Lane (today St. Nicholas Avenue) to race their trotters. And the horseless and carriageless came to the Park to gape at this incredible parade of vehicles and horseflesh.

Some years later the horseflesh gave way to a more personal form of locomotion —the bicycle. High society was hit by the cycling fever and it wasn't an uncommon sight in the 1890's to see a plump Lillian Russell pedalling —on a jewel-studded, gold-plated bicycle— beside an even plumper "Diamond Jim" Brady on the bicycle paths of Central Park.

Meanwhile, the face of New York was changing along with the habits of its citizens. Society was again on the northward march, lining upper Fifth Avenue with French chateaux, Venetian palaces, English manor houses (or combinations thereof) facing fashionable Central Park. And hotels, the ultimate in luxury and elegance, followed the Best People.

The hotels remain —though several have become hotel-apartments partly owned by their tenants. Some of the chateaux and palaces still remain —though their owners long since deserted them for another world (or the more elegant 90's), and they are presently occupied by foreign consulates, institutions and schools. Most, however, have been replaced —or are being replaced— by luxury apartments.

Yet, Central Park continues Central Park. True, the carriage paths have been paved for the horseless carriage. The bicycle paths are the domain of school children. The band concerts are beloved by the white collar worker and avoided by the socialites. There are more statues and more facilities. The park has added, among other things, a lake, a pond, a meer, a zoo, an artificial ice skating rink, a model boathouse. The park is no longer fashionable and it's no longer safe to walk through it after dark unless you want to be robbed or raped. Nonetheless, Central Park remains what it was essentially from the start: a beautiful green haven away from the traffic and fumes and barrenness of Manhattan and an incomparable way to spend a fine afternoon with the kids.

Central Park

To explore Central Park put on your most comfortable walking shoes and bring along your ice or your roller skates, a kite, checkers or chess, a handball, bocci, picnic lunch, what-have-you. You can easily spend a day in Central Park making use of all these things —and never notice how time has slipped by. In the east half of the park, for example, you'll find the following starting from the main entrance at Fifth Avenue and 59th Street:

▪ A **pond** and **bird sanctuary** immediately west of the entrance. If the pond is frozen, this is your chance to try out those ice skates you brought along. However . . .

▪ You may want to try them out at the **Wollman Memorial** just northwest of the pond which acts as an artificial ice skating rink in winter, a roller skating rink from about April 20th to June 15th and September 8th to October 1st. Admission to the general ice skating sessions on weekdays is 50c for adults, 25c for children under 14; on weekends and holidays, 75c for adults, 50c for children. Children under 14, however, are admitted free on Saturdays and on New York City public school vacations and holidays (except Sundays) from 10 a.m. to 12 noon. Roller skating at the rink is free at all times.

▪ Just northwest of the rink is one of the park's most unique and charming facilities, the **Kinderberg Chess**

and Checkers House usually stocked with deeply concentrating citizens trying to figure out their (or their opponent's) next move.

■ Directly east of the players, facing Fifth Avenue —you may enter through the Children's Gate at 64th Street— is the **Arsenal,** at present the home of the New York City Department of Parks. Directly behind it is the **Menagerie,** better known as the Central Park Zoo —no great shakes as far as the animal specimens (about 430) are concerned (the Bronx Zoo has seven times as many) but probably the most popular spot in the park with nearly two million visitors annually. Admission is free and may still include a look at a smoking chimpanzee —though he may have given that up following the Surgeon General's official pronouncement on smoking and cancer— and some wonderfully hammy seals who love nothing better than an audience.

■ North of the menagerie, on Fifth Avenue, children flock to the park's most recent newcomer —the **Children's Zoo** with smaller, petable and feedable baby animals. The zoo also holds free story-telling sessions using motion pictures or color slides weekdays at 3.30 p.m. and Saturdays at 11 a.m. The Children's Zoo is open daily from 10 a.m. to 5 p.m. but you must be accompanied by a child. Childless adults are only admitted on Mondays. Admission is 10c.

■ West of the Children's Zoo stretches the handsome forty-foot wide esplanade known as the **Mall.** At the northern end of its 1500 foot length, the Mall widens and becomes a concert ground where during the summer months you may hear free band concerts. Check with the Arsenal (Regent 4-1000) for the time and schedule.

■ At the northern end of the Mall, steps lead to a terrace and restaurant overlooking the Park's irregular,

The Children's Zoo at Central Park gets its share of adults

main **Lake.** Broad steps lead past the grandiose Bethesda Fountain down to the lake shore. To the right is the **Loeb Memorial Boathouse** where you may rent a rowboat —unless the boathouse's 300 are already out which, on a lovely day, is quite possible. Charge for the use of the rowboat is 45c per hour, 15c for each additional person and you must leave a $2.00 deposit.

■ Immediately north of the Lake spreads the **Ramble,** the "wildest" part of the park threaded with winding paths and trails and providing a delightful and comparatively cool ramble on a hot summer day.

■ East of the boathouse sparkles the trim **Conservatory Pond** where you and your children may sail (or watch sail) model sailboats. In the companion **Krebs Memorial**

Boathouse you may dry dock your model sailboat (provided it's under 72 inches) for an annual fee of $2. On the western and northern ends of the pond are two recent additions to the rather large statuary population of Central Park: the first is the **Hans Christian Andersen Memorial;** the second, an **Alice-in-Wonderland** group which children may clamber over and be their own rough selves to their heart's content.

- North of the Conservatory Pond, stretching between 80th and 84th Streets, stands that magnificent institution, the **Metropolitan Museum of Art** —but more about this later. Immediately west of the museum stands the park's most famous and oldest monument —the **Obelisk,** more commonly called (for no good reason) Cleopatra's Needle, dating from *circa* 1500 B.C., a gift of the Egyptian Government to the City of New York.

- North of the museum, a huge **Receiving Reservoir** covers nearly the entire width of the park from 86th to 96th Streets —more than 100 acres. It stores water from Westchester County and upstate mountain lakes.

- North beyond the reservoir and the park's East Meadow, with its entrance at 105th Street, blooms the formal and charming **Conservatory Garden** with seasonal displays of flowers.

- Finally, taking up the northeast corner of the park is **Harlem Meer** where you may go rowing. The 110th Street boathouse has 100 rowboats for rent at the same rates as at the main lake (see above).

The west side of the park is mostly devoted to great open rolling meadows and playgrounds, but it too has its special facilities.

- Occupying the southwest corner of the park, extending from 61st to 65th Streets, is the **Heckscher Playground** with the usual playground facilities including a hugely popular, large wading pool and, on its northeastern corner, the **Freidsam Memorial Merry-go-Round.**

■ On Central Park West and 66th Street stands the rustic **Tavern on the Green,** a restaurant-nightclub featuring continuous dancing to two orchestras, a large outdoor and indoor dining area and a most pleasant atmosphere. The Tavern was developed from an 1870 structure known as the sheepfold built to house a flock of sheep assigned the task of keeping the grass in the large meadow north of the building trimmed. The sheep have long since gone to greener pastures but the **Sheep Meadow** (as it is still called) and its grass (trimmed despite the lack of sheep) are still there for you to roll in, play ball in, etc. North, on the west side of the Lake at the level of 72nd Street, children 16 years or younger may fish from April to November.

■ Beyond the Ramble at about the level of 79th Streets stands the **Swedish School House** (a replica of one) which the Department of Parks' Marionette Theater uses as a workshop to make the marionettes, costumes, scenery, etc. for the puppet shows which it puts on free throughout the late spring and summer in New York City's parks. In Central Park the shows are usually put on in mid May and June. For the time and place (which vary), contact the Department of Parks' Marionette Theater at Regent 4-1000. Admission to the show is free.

■ Directly east of the schoolhouse blooms the **Shakespeare Garden,** a formal garden containing all the flowers and plants mentioned in the bard's works plus an oak tree imported from Stratford-on-Avon.

■ Appropriately, close by stands the new **Shakespeare Outdoor Theater** where —after a good deal of haggling with former Park Commissioner Robert Moses— each summer Joseph Papp presents generally excellent productions of Shakespeare's plays. *Shakespeare-in-the-Park,* as the repertory theater has come to be known, is free but extremely popular. If you want to find seats among the 2300 of the amphitheater where you can see and clearly hear the actors, you had best arrive a good hour or so before the curtain (figuratively speaking) goes up. For a schedule of the programs consult the entertainment section of the daily newspapers or call the Department of Parks.

▪ Acting as a backdrop to Shakespeare-in-the-Park is **Belvedere,** a medieval castle-like affair housing meteorological instruments maintained by the United States Weather Bureau. The park's **New Lake** stretches eastward from the theater. To its north spreads the inviting **Great Lawn,** periodic scene of soccer games, softball and baseball games. Between 94th and 101st Streets are the **South** and **North Meadows** with 30 tennis courts in the first and a baseball diamond in the second. The latter also has handball courts and three soccer fields.

▪ North of North Meadow a pool flows into a lovely loch which in turn flows into the Harlem Meer. Lastly, beyond the loch at the northern edge of the park by the Seventh Avenue (Warrior's) Gate, a venerable block house has been standing there since colonial days.

Finally, scattered throughout the park, usually around the periphery, are some 25 or so children's playgrounds with the usual complement of see-saws, slides, swings, jungle gyms, parallel and horizontal bars, etc.

Upper Fifth Avenue

So much for the park, itself. Its surroundings are never as pleasant, but they enfold a multitude of things some of them quite interesting. Begin first by following the path that High Society blazed —beyond the glittering, smart Fifth Avenue shops from 59th to 110th Streets.

First a word about that respected and *recherché*

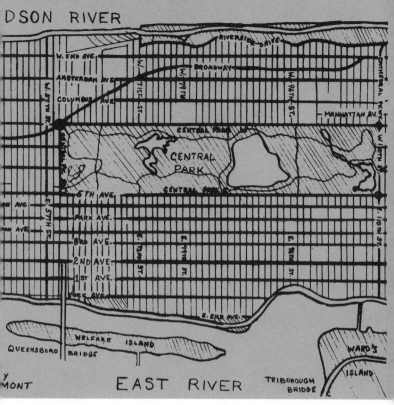

hostelry on the southwest corner of 59th Street and Fifth Avenue, the Plaza Hotel, a landmark there since it was opened in 1907. Though some of its facilities —the gilded, grilled elevators and the old fashion plumbing, for example— tend to reflect its more than half a century, and though it may have been passed in plushness and luxury by such near neighbors as the 1930 Hotel Pierre (diagonally across the way at Fifth Avenue and 61st Street), the Plaza retains the elegant air of the days when the Vanderbilts and the Harrimans engaged suites for its opening season. The old aristocracy still clings to it in preference to the more showy Johnny-come-latelies and its not uncommon to catch a glimpse of Cary Grant or some other movie star waiting, like other mortals, for one of its gilded elevators. Incidentally, the Plaza is just one in a long row of luxury hotels lining Central Park South from Fifth to Seventh Avenues.

Grand Army Plaza

The Plaza Hotel is so called because it overlooks Grand Army Plaza extending from 58th to 60th Street. Directly in front of the hotel, on the south side of the plaza, flows the Pulitzer Memorial Fountain (one of the few fountains in the city) topped by the delectable statue of a feminine —and nude— "Abundance" designed by Karl Ritter. Across the way, Saint-Gaudens' statue of General William Tecumseh Sherman, lead by a young miss ("Victory"), perpetually tries to cross 59th Street traffic to bathe in the waters of Abundance —but never seems to make any headway.

Patiently standing on the south side of 59th Street and the plaza, you'll find a remnant of a bygone era: an ancient horse and carriage, shiny black with red upholstery, and a generally top-hatted coachman offering a leisurely and bumpety ride through Central Park —if you care to stand the pace and the stiff fee (maximum of $5.00 for the first half hour, $2.00 for each additional half hour or fraction thereof).

Walking northward on Fifth Avenue you will come upon the stately Temple Emanu-El, standing at the corner of 65th Street, the largest and most magnificent synagogue in New York City with the oldest reform congregation (founded in 1845 by a group of wealthy German Jews). The temple, itself, superbly simple, dates from 1930.

At 68th Street, two blocks east to Park Avenue, stands Hunter College (established in 1870), the world's largest educational institution for women with a student body of about 5000. (In its Bronx annex, though, the college succumbed to social pressure and permits the male intruder.) Hunter is just one of the seven colleges comprising the City University of New York, the world's largest municipal university with an enrollment of about 90,000 matriculated and non-matriculated students.

Frick Museum

Continuing north again on Fifth Avenue, at the corner of 70th Street, you'll find one of New York City's most distinguished art museums —the Frick Collection. The building, a gem, —the former palace (it had over 100 rooms) of Henry Clay Frick, Andrew Carnegie's associate— is an outstanding example of the Age of Conspicuous Consumption. The collection —primarily of 14th to 19th century paintings— is displayed not as though it were in a museum but rather in the private home —elegantly furnished with French, Italian and English period furniture— of someone with superb taste in art and the wherewithal to satisfy it. The collection, by art museum standards, is not large but what there is of it is excellent. It includes paintings by Bellini, Titian, Tintoretto, Holbein, Hals, Van Dyck, Rembrandt, Vermeer, El Greco, Velazquez, Goya, Boucher, Fragonard, Monet, Renoir, Hogarth, Gainsborough, Reynolds, Constable, Turner, Whistler and others. Illustrated lectures on the collection are given on Wednesdays, Thursdays and Fridays at 3 p.m.

The Frick Collection is open free Tuesdays through Saturdays from 10 a.m. to 5 p.m. and Sundays and holidays from 1 to 5 p.m. One unhappy (but reasonable) note: children under 10 years are not admitted; children under 16 are admitted only if accompanied by an adult.

Metropolitan Museum of Art

A dozen blocks north of the Frick Collection on the West side of Fifth Avenue stands another superb (there is no other word for it unless it's stupendous) art museum —the Metropolitan Museum of Art. Perhaps too supendous should be the term for where the Frick concentrated on quality but in a limited range, the Metropolitan offers not only quality but quantity, variety and a range spreading over more than 5000 years of art. The result has been one of the world's truly great art collections and the finest museum of its kind in the Western Hemisphere —one that will give you museum fright just from its magnitude.

The museum's collection is housed in a mammoth building, three stories high, stretching from 82nd to 86th Street. It will take you a full day's work (albeit pleasurable) to examine carefully just one wing so don't even think of covering it all in one day. How can you expect to see in one visit Greecian urns, the head of Queen Hatshepsut, knights in armor, Benvenuto Cellini's exquisite Rospigliosi Cup, the entire tomb of an Egyptian noble, Assyrian sculptures, El Greco's View of Toledo, more than 30 great Rembrandt's (including his *Aristotle Contemplating the Bust of Homer,* purchased by the museum at the highest price ever paid for a painting —$2,300,000), have lunch at a cafeteria whose focal point is a charming fountain with sprite-like sculptures by Sweden's great Carl Milles, and so on —all at widely divergent points?

Then there are the Costume Institute and the special exhibits, lectures and concerts (the latter have included performances by such music notables as Nathan Milstein, Julian Bream, the Budapest String Quartet, all within the space of a fortnight), the special children's programs and classes, which are very much a part of the Metropolitan.

Where knighthood is in flower: the Metropolitan Museum of Art

The museum is open every day in the year (admission free) though you may find some of its sections closed on Christmas Day and, in a few cases, on Saturdays and Sundays as well. The hours are from 10 a.m. to 5 p.m. Mondays through Saturdays; 1 to 5 p.m. Sundays and holidays. Its cafeteria —and you should try it at least once just for the Carl Milles fountain— is open for luncheon Mondays through Saturdays from 11:30 a.m. to 2:30 p.m. and Sundays from 12 noon to 3 p.m.

The Guggenheim Museum

The Solomon Guggenheim Museum, just two blocks north of the Metropolitan Museum of Art, at 1071 Fifth Avenue (the corner of 88th Street), is as different from the latter as night from day, starting with the building designed by that Dean of Architectural Individualism, Frank Lloyd Wright. Whether you approve of the building's design or not you'll have to admit that it is vastly different from any other you've ever seen. In the words of its architect, it is "one great space of continuous floor" —a quarter of a mile long ramp rising in a spiral for six floors to a height of 92 feet. The paintings are hung in bays (43 of them) arranged to follow the gentle sweep of the spiral.

A list of the painters represented in the Guggenheim Museum sounds like the "Who's Who" of Modern Art. The collection ranges anywhere from Impressionism to abstract expressionism. It holds the world's largest museum collection of paintings by Vasily Kandinsky and New York City's largest museum collection of sculptures by Constantin Brancusi.

The museum opens its doors Tuesdays through Saturdays from 10 a.m. to 6 p.m. (except Thursdays when it is open until 9 p.m.) and Sundays and holidays from 12 noon to 6 p.m. It is closed Mondays (except Labor

Day), Christmas Day and July 4th. Admission is 50c. Children under 6 years are admitted free.

Then, continue your stroll along famous Fifth. At 91st Street stands the former $3 million, 64-room mansion of Andrew Carnegie, held on to stubbornly by his widow until her death though the building's extensive garden (covering nearly half a block) cost her in taxes alone more than seven times the annual income of a middle class wage earner. Today the Carnegie home houses the New York School of Social Work of Columbia University. It still has the large pipe organ that Carnegie had installed and the Scotsman's Scottish oak desk in his former study.

The Jewish Museum

One block north at the northeast corner of 92nd Street stands another unique institution: the Jewish Museum, caretaker of the world's largest and most comprehensive collection of Jewish ceremonial objects and of historical Judaica. The museum was started in 1904 as an adjunct to the library of the Jewish Theological Seminary of America. It was the proud owner of 26 ceremonials. Today just one part of its collection —the Friedman collection— has more than 5000 objects and it is now housed in the former Felix M. Warburg mansion (a gift from his widow) and the recently added Albert A. List Building adjoining.

With the additional space at its disposal, the museum broadened its scope to display the work of contemporary artists as yet unrecognized by the community. A Gallery Talk is given Wednesdays at 3 p.m. on the contemporary art exhibit, followed at 4 p.m. by a talk on the Judaic exhibit. The museum is open Mondays through Wednesdays from 12 noon to 5 p.m., Thursdays to 9 p.m. and Sundays from 11 a.m. to 6 p.m. Admission is free.

Museum of the City of New York

Further north on Fifth Avenue, at No. 1220 (filling the block front from 103rd to 104th Street), stands a jewel of a museum which, unfortunately, too many New Yorkers ignore —don't even know exists— though it is their very own, maintained in part by their taxes, viz., the Museum of the City of New York, housed in a Georgian style building of red and white brick. For anyone with the slightest interest in New York City, this museum is a must; for children —or anyone with a child's curiosity and uncomplicated heart, the museum is a delight. You'll find on permanent exhibit alcoves showing the costumes and furnishings used in the various periods of New York's history; a 17th century Dutch kitchen, silver, furniture, ship models, a marine gallery, fire engines, prints, photographs and maps, toys (prize newcomer: a recently donated collection of 38 antique dolls from the mid 18th to mid 19th century, including "Mehitabel Hodges," a doll imported from France in 1724), plus small scale models recreating almost 450 years of the city's history.

The museum also features in its auditorium one-hour long puppet shows, put on by professional puppeteers, every Saturday from October through June at 1:30 p.m. Admission to the puppet shows is 50c for children under 15, $1.00 for those 15 and over. From October through mid-May, on Sundays between 3 and 4 p.m., the museum also sponsors concerts featuring talented students from New York City's music schools. Admission to these family concerts is free. Finally, on alternate Sundays from April to October (weather permitting), the museum sponsors "Walking Tours" of New York City's best known neighborhoods with a knowledgeable guide who knows his New York City history —and his way around. Price of the tours is $2.50 for a single ticket or

$7.50 for four tickets either to a single tour or to four different tours or to any combination thereof. The Walking Tours meet at 2:30 p.m. at designated locations depending upon the neighborhood to be explored and reservations should (preferably) be made in advance. For further details contact the museum's development office at LE 4-1672.

The museum is open, admission free, Tuesdays through Saturdays from 10 a.m. to 5 p.m.; Sundays from 1 to 5 p.m. It is closed Mondays and Christmas Day.

Down by the River

A few blocks east of Fifth Avenue, the luxurious mansions dwindle down to nothing but you'll still find some interesting buildings to see. Down at 421 East 61st Street, among otherwise uninspired neighbors stands one of New York City's oldest houses —a trim colonial affair, first built as a carriage house and then, in 1799, converted into the home of Colonel William S. Smith, son-in-law of President John Adams. In 1925, partly because they were in need of a clubhouse, but mostly because they wanted to preserve this fine example of colonial days, the Colonial Dames of America purchased the house and property and set up housekeeping in it. The house is furnished as it must have been in the early 19th century and the Colonial Dames hope to be able to stay in their colonial home indefinitely despite the building ague which has afflicted this part of town. The Dames open their doors to the public Mondays through Fridays from 10 a.m. to 4 p.m., admission free.

In distinct contrast to the Smith House, is the huge medical group of buildings, extending from 68th to 71st Street on York Avenue, which includes the New York Hospital-Cornell Medical Center and the Memorial Center for Cancer and Allied Diseases. The hospital, chartered in 1771, was New York's first. The Cornell Medical Center, opened in 1932, includes the Cornell University Medical School and the School for Nurses. The famed Sloan-Kettering Research Institute and several hospitals specializing in cancer research, treatment and prevention, comprise the Memorial Center for Cancer and Allied Diseases.

Little Germany

At one time not so long ago the section above 71st Street as far north as 89th Street and extending as far west as Third Avenue was one of the most colorful of New York —a slice of little old Europe where the Bohemians (not the ones of Greenwich Village but the native or second generation Bohemians from Bohemia), the Hungarians, the Czechs and the Germans congregated. The building boom, however, has reached this part of town, too —especially around the southern section— and many a quaint and inexpensive restaurant and café have been replaced by luxury apartments. Even so, Yorkville, from 83rd to 89th Street, the little Germany of New York City, still retains most of its *beirstubes* and *brauhauses,* its *wurst, sauerbraten* and potato dumplings with a liberal dash of dancing and singing and hoopla —especially along 86th Street, Little Germany's Pigalle.

Gracie Mansion

Down on 89th Street by the East River, on the northern end of Carl Schurz Park (named after Lincoln's ambassador to Spain), the Mayor and his family can watch from Gracie Mansion the tugs and other river craft that make their way past the narrow sliver of Welfare Island. Spacious, spreading Gracie Mansion, the official residence of New York City's mayors since 1942 has been standing in that spot since 1799 when it was built (in the Federal style of the day) for Archibald Gracie, a wealthy (and retiring) merchant. The mansion has been spruced up since then and elegantly furnished with period pieces on loan from the city's museums, etc. The mayor's home, alas, is not open to the public except, on rare occasions, by special appointment and usually only to groups.

The West Side Story

West of Central Park the atmosphere becomes decidedly less rarefied though at one time real estate speculators dreamed of establishing another "gold front" like that along Fifth Avenue along the extension of Eighth Avenue (Central Park West) facing the park. Those dreams never materialized though some of our more distinguished citizens do continue to live as west siders. In general, the section —in particular that west of Broadway— deteriorated into seedy looking slums with row upon row of brownstone houses. It became extremely difficult to believe that at one time the area was the lovely farm district the early Dutch called *Bloemendaal* or Bloomingdale (vale of flowers).

Nonetheless, west side real estate owners are back again to dreaming. The west is presently undergoing "improvement pains" and the hopes are that some of the projects —primarily the new Lincoln Center for the Performing Arts— will give new tone to this down-at-the-heels section. Time will tell. Meanwhile the west side of Central Park still has its own brand of attractions.

Columbus Circle

Your stroll along the west side should start at Columbus Circle where Eighth Avenue converges with Broadway as Eighth and leaves the northern end of the circle as Central Park West. Presiding over this busy intersection and its traffic (which after some recent improvements seems to be running more smoothly), stands a statue of Christopher Columbus perched high on a slender column in the center of the circle. The statue was erected there in 1892 to commemorate the 400th anniversary of the discovery of the New World.

Facing the northeast quadrant of the circle at its entrance to Central Park, is the Maine Memorial dedicated to those who lost their lives when the battleship Maine was sunk in Havana harbor. Though it doesn't appear to have much connecting it with the sinking of the Maine, the memorial represents "Columbia Triumphant" —and Columbia, standing on top of the monumental base, her seashell chariot and team of three seahorses were cast from a cannon raised from the sunken ship.

New York Coliseum

Occupying the block front between 58th and 60th Streets, facing Columbus Circle, spreads a modern building which —with some reason— bills itself as "the world's greatest showcase" and "the exposition capital of the world." The New York Coliseum, built at a cost of $35 million, has more than 300,000 square feet of modern, air conditioned exhibition space. In one year an average 3 million people (New Yorkers as well as visitors from all over the world) can be expected to stop at the Coliseum to see some 30 different major expositions. In the space of three months, for example, this mammoth exposition hall was the scene of the annual National Motor Boat Show, a "Start Your Own Business" exposition, the National Sports, Vacation and Travel Show, an Antique Fair and Sale, an International Flower Show, the annual International Automotive Show, etc.

New York Coliseum and . . .

. . . the Maine Memorial

Shows held at the Coliseum are well advertised in the newspapers, over the radio, etc. —you can hardly avoid knowing what's on. Price of admission, if any, varies depending upon the exposition being presented.

Behind the Coliseum, old brownstone houses have been replaced by modern new apartment buildings. Occupying the entire two blocks from 60th to 62nd Street, between Columbus Avenue (the extension of Ninth Avenue beyond 57th Street) and Amsterdam Avenue (the extension of Tenth Avenue), stands Fordham University's new 7½ acre campus which, when completed, will have cost $25½ million and, together with the neighboring Lincoln Center, will comprise one of the world's most important cultural and educational centers.

Lincoln Center for the Performing Arts

North of Fordham University, occupying the blocks from 62nd Street to 66th Streets, between Columbus and Amsterdam Avenues, clusters that most welcome newcomer to New York City's cultural scene, the Lincoln Center for the Performing Arts —in various stages of construction. First building in the group to be completed was **Philharmonic Hall,** permanent home of the New York Philharmonic Orchestra and its inexhaustible, young conductor Leonard Bernstein. For the first time in its 121-year history, the Philharmonic played to a completely sold out audience during the entire first season at its new home. Air conditioning permits a year-round season at the Hall, an innovation for music-loving New Yorkers who heretofore during the summer had to go outdoors —the Lewisohm Stadium Concerts or the band concerts in the park— or out of town (Tanglewood, Mass.) for their music.

The second building to be completed, the **New York State Theater,** started its first season to coincide with the official opening of the 1964-1965 New York World's Fair —April 23rd, 1964. It is the new headquarters for a New York City pride and joy —the comparatively young but excellent New York City Ballet under the expert and imaginative direction of George Ballanchine. The New York City Ballet left its old dancing grounds at the City Center (on invitation from the Lincoln Center) for a two year trial period (40 weeks of performances) during which time both the Center and the ballet company will see how things work out.

The New York State Theater also shelters a newcomer to New York's entertainment scene —the **Music Theater of Lincoln Center** which, under the leadership of Richard Rodgers, will stage the Center's lighter entertainment —operettas and musical comedies. In addition, other American and foreign companies (for example, the Royal Shakespeare Theater from England) will make special appearances at the State Theater from time to time.

The remaining buildings of the Lincoln Center still to be completed are:

■ The new, air conditioned **Metropolitan Opera House** scheduled to be completed in late 1965. When completed the building, rising 14 stories high, with its horseshoe shaped auditorium of red, gold and ivory and its tiers of boxes, will be able to seat 3750 (about 150 more than the old) and will hold, in addition, three restaurants. Best of all, the façade with its five towering arches will be a vast improvement over the old stone-face at 39th Street and Broadway.

■ The **Library-Museum of the Performing Arts** and the **Vivian Beaumont Theater** scheduled to be completed in 1965. The library-museum will house the New York Public Library's extensive archives on music, the theater and the dance. The Vivian Beaumont Theater will be the home of New York City's new Repertory Theater under the joint leadership of Robert Whitehead and Elia Kazan.

The last building in the Lincoln Center group, not scheduled for completion until 1967, is the Julliard School of Music and Lincoln Center Chamber Music Hall whose construction must await the demolition of a city high school on the site at present.

You make take a guided one-hour tour of the Lincoln Center for the Performing Arts —what's completed of it— conducted by the Center's Visitors Services. The tours which leave approximately every 15 minutes or so (daily) cost $1.25 for adults; 75c for children; groups of 10 or more, $1.00 per adult, 60c per student. For further information call TR 4-4010.

New York Historical Society

North at 77th Street and Central Park West, in a dignified neo-classic building, the venerable New York Historical Society (organized in 1804 and the second oldest historical society in the United States) proceeds about its business of collecting fascinating and detailed memorabilia of New York City's history —past, present and future. The society, which maintains one of our country's finest libraries and museums of American history, is an old friend to historians and scholars but, unfortunately for them, the average New Yorker may pass the building hundreds of times during the year and never once drop in to see the many interesting displays.

You'll want, for example, to see the society's wonderful collection of watercolors by the one and only John James Audubon and the exhibit on the history of New York City traced through paintings, prints and ship models arranged in a gallery set up as the deck and cabin of a sailing ship. Then there are the bedroom and parlor from Mount Pleasant, the Beekman family home which served as British headquarters during the American Revolution and where Nathan Hale was tried as a spy and sentenced to be hanged; a display of early American arts and crafts including pewter and painted powder horns; an extensive collection of early American paintings and sculptures (including four by Daniel Chester French); a fascinating gallery on New York City's Volunteer Fire Department with early hand-drawn fire engines and models of early fire-fighting machines. You'll chuckle over the fire alarm box with its key available (as the sign reads) "at the Saloon."

On Saturdays at 11:30 p.m., the museum also shows free films (both features and documentaries) —usually an American film classic or a film depicting some aspect of American history or the American scene. If you're there in February, for example, you may be able to watch "Young Mr. Lincoln" starring Henry Fonda. In winter the museum's offerings include free, varied one-hour concerts (ranging anywhere from chamber music to folk music) beginning at 2:30 p.m. Finally, the museum has an extra soft heart for children: it often puts on famous children's film classics —Gulliver's Travels, for example— or puppet shows or music concerts and for more than ten years the museum has been delighting the neighborhood children with a Story Hour Friday mornings in July. Admission to the Society's exhibits and events is free at all times. However, because the puppet shows are so popular and the space is limited, you must procure tickets for them in advance. Write to the Society's Supervisor of Education or telephone TR 3-3400.

The Society's library is also open to adults (for research) daily except Sundays from 10 a.m. to 5 p.m. and holidays from 1 to 5 p.m. The art gallery and museum are open daily except Mondays from 1 to 5 p.m. but on Saturdays open at 10 a.m. The entire building is closed New Year's Day, Memorial Day, Fourth of July, Labor Day, Thanksgiving and Christmas Day and all during the month of August when, like sensible people, everyone goes someplace where it's cool.

American Museum of Natural History

Next door to the New York Historical Society, in a rambling maze of buildings, spreads one of the world's truly great museums —the sprawling American Museum of Natural History and its star-bright companion, the Hayden Planetarium. President Ulysses S. Grant laid the cornerstone for the museum in 1874 but so many buildings have ben added since then (there are 19 of them all told) that the musem's staff doesn't know exactly where to find the cornerstone. Inside these buildings, 58 great halls and alcoves hold more than 2300 habitat groups, dioramas, scientific exhibits, etc., behind four acres of glass. And this only represents one tenth of the museum's scientific treasures for it has tens of millions of zoological, geological, anthropological and botanical specimens locked in its cavernous (and insect- and dust-proof)vaults.

How do you go about seeing such an inexhaustible fount of natural wonders? Like the Metropolitan Museum of Art, you don't try to see it all in one day —it can't be done, at least, not satisfactorily. The first step is to arm yourself with a floor plan of the museum (available from any of the attendants). Another good arm is a little booklet entitled "General Guide to the Exhibits" which is available at the museum's shop on the first floor near the 77th Street entrance and is one of the best 25c buys you'll find in Manhattan. If your time is limited, check the list of exhibits and decide upon perhaps ten which you would like to see above all others. To do the exhibits full justice, that should take a good four or five hours of your enthralled attention (with time off for lunch). By that time your head will be reeling —and your feet aching.

Interests vary but certainly you shouldn't leave the museum without, for example, seeing on the fourth floor, in the Hall of Early Dinosaurs, that awesome collection of mounted bones —a fierce, carnivorous *allosaurus,* smaller but deadly, stalking the huge (66-foot long, 18-foot high) but inoffensive and herbivorous *brontosaurus* (also known as the "Thunder Lizard," because when the 40-ton reptile walked, his footsteps sounded like thunder). Or, on the same floor in the Hall of Late Dinosaurs, *Tyrannosaurus rex,* 20 feet tall and 45 feet long, the king of the flesh-eating dinosaurs.

Tyrannosaurus rex
in the Hall of Late Dinosaurs
American Museum of Natural History

Other outstanding exhibits include:

■ The group of African mammals (on the second and third floors) —including a herd of seven elephants which seem to be thundering through the center of the great hall— all incredibly life-like in settings realistically duplicating their natural habitats.

■ A wonderful collection of "Birds of the World" on the second floor and of North American Birds on the third floor.

■ The Men of the Montaña Hall on the second floor showing community life among a group of South American Indians living in a rain forest of the Andes (complete with the sounds of the forests).

■ The mineral and gem collection on the fourth floor which includes among other gems the "Star of India," the largest star sapphire in the world, and an exquisite crystal carving of Atlas with his legendary burden on his shoulders.

■ The museum also has a natural Science Center for Young Children devoted to informal exhibits on the wild life and geology of metropolitan New York. (The hours the Center is open vary considerably depending upon the month and the day. For further information, call TR 3-1300, ext. 281.)

In addition to its exhibits, the museum offers free gallery and slide lectures for adults during the fall and spring, as well as free motion pictures on Wednesdays (for adults only) and on Saturdays (for both adults and children) from October to May at 2 p.m. You may obtain the museum's free Calendar of Events from a guard.

■ The Hayden Planetarium

No visit is complete to the American Museum of Natural History without taking in one of the "sky programs" given several times each day at the Hayden Planetarium, the museum's Department of Astronomy. On the 75-foot in diameter dome of the planetarium, a Zeiss projector faithfully reproduces the stars, planets, sun and moon as seen from any point in the world depending upon the whim of the operator (and the program scheduled). The operator can, for example, show you the sky over Bethlehem on Christmas Eve 1964 years ago or he can show you how New York City's sky will look 12,000 years from now with the southern cross shining overhead. The planetarium, besides, has many fascinating exhibits on astronomy, space exploration and celestial phenomena.

For the latter exhibits, a dramatic "black light" technique —glowing fluorescent pigments against a black background— is used to produce a striking, almost three-dimensional effect.

Price of admission to the Hayden Planetarium's matinees is $1.00 for adults and 50c for children over five. (Children under five are not admitted.) For the evening programs add another 25c to the above price.

The American Museum of Natural History is open every day of the year, admission free, from 10:00 a.m. to 5:00 p.m. on weekdays and from 1:00 p.m. to 5:00 p.m. on Sundays and holidays.

North of the mueseum, the area extending roughly to 110th Street between Amsterdam and West End Avenues —once a slum— is rapidly giving way to new housing developments. However, let's hope that the quaint Victorian London lane between 94th and 95th Streets and limited by Broadway and West End will not succumb to progress. The lane is called Pomander Walk (after a play from the early 1900's) and, in fact, was inspired by the stage setting for that play. Theater notables —Madeleine Carroll, Nancy Carroll, Louis Wolheim among them— once called the cottages on the Walk home.

Riverside Drive and Park

Down on the west side by the Hudson River, starting at 72nd Street and extending to the northern end of Manhattan, runs a narrow strip of green known (at least, as far as 125th Street) as Riverside Park. Riverside Drive accompanies it on its northward course until it merges with the Henry Hudson Parkway and runs off Manhattan. Both Park and Drive afford one of the pleasantest outings on this rock-bound island. The wide promenade along the river gives you a breezy chance to watch the boats steaming up the mighty Hudson and to note the activity and the palisades on the Jersey side. On meandering Riverside Drive you may drive slowly and enjoy the view and the river coolness without having a car hurrying you from behind. (Cars in a hurry can zoom by overhead on the Henry Hudson Parkway.)

At 79th Street, a lovely Gothic rotunda (under a cloverleaf of the Henry Hudson Parkway) with a fountain and wading pool gives you a perfect excuse for taking off your shoes and socks and wiggling your toes —delightful, especially for tourist-tired feet. At 82nd and 92nd Streets, you'll find a chance to fish all year round.

At one time the Henry Hudson River along this stretch was to have been another Rhine, surmounted by the castles and chateaux of the wealthy and aristocratic. For some reason, the west somehow never quite made the grade, and though the Drive continues to be an affluent neighborhood, most of society abandoned their mansions in the west for their little gray shacks in the east. In consequence, their homes were converted into apartment houses and today many a humbler folk instead enjoy the incomparable view of the Hudson and the coolest spot on Manhattan during the dog days of August.

Riverside Drive, incidentally, is dotted with monuments. At 89th Street stands the Soldiers and Sailors Monument —a colonaded, smaller, slenderer, esthetically more pleasing structure than the more famous Grant's Tomb further north. The monument was erected in honor of the Union soldiers that died during the the Civil War. North on 93rd Street, a militant, mounted Joan of Arc brandishes her sword over Riverside Drive. Stones from the Rouen Tower, where she was held prisoner before being burned at the stake, and from the Reims Cathedral, where the king she placed on the throne of France was crowned, have been incorporated into the pedestal of her monument.

As a fitting end to your Riverside stroll, visit the little Ne Yu Koku (New York) Buddhist Church at 171 West 94th Street, founded more than a quarter of a century ago and still flourishing. The church has an interesting traditional shrine of black enamel, gold and lacquer imported from Kyoto with incense burners and lotus blossoms and other exotic appurtenances. The Buddhist high priest of this little church (and his wife) have set up classes in flower arrangements and in Japanese art to attract people to his little flock. They will also give you free lessons on how to speak Japanese. If you happen to be passing by in spring, likely as not you will be able to see their annual flower arrangement exhibit.

The Feast of Obon

Best of all, if you're in New York toward the end of July, chances are you'll be able to watch the Japanese, (they come from all over New York and Toronto) as they celebrate, down at Riverside Park and 103rd Street, the Feast of *Ullambana* or *Obon* when, according to their beliefs, the souls of the dead return and are reunited for a few brief hours with those they loved on earth. On that day you will see the celebrants in richly colorful Japanese costumes going through a stately ceremonial dance to the sound of gongs and ritual drums while men, women and children sing in chorus. Above them the park will be gay with Japanese paper lanterns and bright streamers waving in the breeze coming up from the river. At the end of the feast, the souls return once again to their heavenly abode while the celebrants return to their homes and put away their ritual robes for another year. And the Hudson and Ne Yu Yoku keep rolling along.

**Rumble? No. A friendly
game of touch football
in a Harlem Street.**

9 | *Harlem*

Section	From 110th Street to Marble Hill.
Map	See page 205.
First stop	*East Side:* IRT-Lexington Avenue to 110th Street — local stop. *West side:* IRT-Broadway to Cathedral Parkway-110th Street — local stop.
Sights for the children	Randall Island, Museum of the American Indian, Jumel Mansion, Fort Washington Park, Jeffrey's Lighthouse underneath the George Washington Bridge, Fort Tyron Park, The Cloisters, Dykeman House, Innwood Hill Park.

id the Hinterland

To most New Yorkers the section above Central Park is one vast, sprawling slum —Harlem— stretching from 110th Street out to the northern tip of Manhattan, only sporadically broken up by a university campus, a stadium or two, a few parks here and there and, oh yes, the Cloisters. (They've heard tell of the last. Few have ever wandered so far into the hinterlands that they can give a first hand account of it —one of New York City's loveliest sights.)

Most New Yorkers prefer to avoid Harlem. They pass it by with averted eyes hoping to ignore the goading prick of uneasy conscience. They stick to their side of Manhattan never venturing beyond Central Park except for an occasional sally into the Harlem night life they've heard so much about. At night, besides, the neon lights of Harlem's Broadway —125th Street— seem to paint the section in a rose colored haze. Things don't look half bad then. It's a pity. It's a pity New Yorkers don't visit this part of their town more often: first, because they might be shamed into doing something about it; secondly, because the northern section of Manhattan —as yet un-leveled by bulldozers— has the most rugged and beautiful terrain of the island.

The Three Harlems

Harlem covers an area roughly extending from the East and Harlem Rivers to Morningside Heights (in some parts almost to the Hudson) and from 110th Street to 155th Street and (more sketchily) beyond. At one time this area was the prosperous middle class village which the early Knickerbockers named after their charming town of Haarlem back in the Old Country. Though by 1874 the corporate limits of New York City had been extended beyond the Harlem River, Harlem remained pretty much of a peaceful farming village. Harlem con-tinued so —sedate and bucolic and prosperous— well into the end of the 19th century often looking with horror and raised eyebrows at the City Steeped in Sin to the south and shaking its disapproving middle class head at the moral and financial extravagances of the downtown multimillionaires.

In 1870 the "Rapid Transit" (steam-driven elevated trains) began its work of disseminating New York City's population, up till then in a congested cluster mostly below 23rd Street. By 1880 three Rapid Transit lines had reached the Harlem River. Real estate speculators (count-ing on past history) and anticipating the northward march of wealth, began constructing costly apartment and town houses in Harlem, convinced the section would blossom into a bastion of the affluent —another Central Park East. Even Stanford White, the architectural darling of New York's society, was commissioned to design some houses for the expected migration of millionaires. But the best laid schemes o' mice an' men gang aft a-gley. Society, having drawn an invisible line at about 100th Street, was not to be enticed from its east side penthouse overlooking the Park.

Meanwhile the Third Avenue El was bringing to these hinterlands the spill over from the Lower East Side, and the face of Harlem which had changed little in two centuries was suddenly transformed. Jewish and Italian immigrants began to settle along east Harlem. Finally, in 1901, the Negro broke the barrier and began moving to this section of town. By 1930, Harlem —now a city within the city— had a population of more than 200,000 and was indisputably the intellectual, artistic and entertainment capital of the Negro world. The white world, in fact, would flock to such popular Harlem night spots as the Cotton Club (where, strangely enough, Negroes were not welcome) and Small's Paradise to hear the new kind of music —jazz and the blues— played by such Negro greats as Duke Ellington, Fletcher Henderson, Cab Calloway, Louis Armstrong, Ethel Waters, etc.

Today, Harlem continues changing. Visitors expecting to find that heady mixture of entertainment, narcotics and crime that attracted the large numbers of slumming parties to this No-Man's Land above Central Park during the 1920's and 30's will be vastly disappointed. Jazz and the blues are no longer novelties but, rather, respected institutions accepted and enjoyed by highbrow and lowbrow alike. They are, in fact, commodities which oft times

Spanish Harlem's market stalls sell anything from layettes to Café Bustelo

can best be found outside Harlem: Carnegie and Philharmonic Halls, for example, and fashionable Basin Street East or the Embers in the east 50's, Birdland on Broadway, Nick's in the Village or the Metropole on Broadway in the 40's, the last two institutions from the days when jazz first set New York on fire in the 1910's.

Even the musical beat of Harlem is changing: the strum of the big bass fiddle has been replaced by the soft shic of the *maracas*. So is the color changing, for the various shades of browns and whites of the Puerto Rican have overrun the once almost entirely black domain.

▪ Italian Harlem

There is as yet a small strip between Lexington Avenue to the East River and from 96th to 125th Streets where Italian immigrants, fleeing the overcrowded conditions of the Lower East Side, once settled and have remained. Here you may still buy pizza and provolone and Italian sausages by the yard, and aging paesani still roll bocci in Thomas Jefferson Park by the river. But the strip is getting smaller all the time. The Italians are slowly losing ground to the Puerto Ricans from the west and the housing developments on the east. On the Feast of Our Lady of Mount Carmel —heretofore an Italian street festival lasting the week of July 16th— the sounds of *merengues, mambos* and *pachangas* are borne on the same air laden with the delicious smells of Italian cooking.

▪ Spanish Harlem

The real poverty-stricken Harlem —Spanish Harlem— extends roughly between Lexington and Fifth Avenue from 96th Street to the Harlem River and beyond. The demarcation lines are by no means sharp for the Puerto Rican continues spilling over on all four sides. Here, in incredibly crowded, deplorable quarters, live the bulk of Manhattan's some 300,000 Puerto Ricans. Since the Second World War huge numbers deserted the blue skies, sun and poverty of their emerald island to look for opportunity in this land of opportunity. They found instead gray skies, filthy, uninhabitable tenements and prejudice and resentment. Where juvenile delinquency and gangland "rumbles" were unheard of in Puerto Rico, in Puerto Rican Harlem they have become commonplace.

One of the most colorful parts of this depressing area are the public market stalls along upper Park Avenue bursting at the seams with everything from layettes to Café Bustelo. You'll find an exotic array of foods

—*yuca, plátanos, mangos,* Spanish sausages— you won't find in your supermarket. You'll also find along this section small luncheonettes and restaurants serving some exciting dishes which, if you're adventuresome and reasonably healthy gastrically speaking, you may find enjoyable. Try *carne mechada* (a deliciously condimented pot roast), *mofongo* (a combination of mashed *plátanos* —a cooking banana— and pork) and chicharrón (fried pork rinds).

■ **Negro Harlem**

West of Spanish Harlem, Negro Harlem extends down almost to the Hudson River. The poorest section of Negro Harlem is a step higher on the social (and economic) scale than Spanish Harlem. The affluent residents of Negro Harlem, however, —the doctors, lawyers, engineers, physicists, etc., living in cliffside homes along the western face of Morningside Heights or overlooking Central Park North or along Edgecombe and St. Nicholas Avenues and Hamilton Terrace or in the homes designed by Stanford White along 138th and 139th Streets— have finer homes, larger incomes and more impressive college degrees than the majority of the whites living on the "right" side of 110th Street.

■ **125th Street and The Apollo**

Traversing the three Harlems —in fact, the "Great White Way" of the entire section— is 125th Street, an almost unbroken row of cafés, restaurants, bars, eating spots, shops and theaters. One of these —the Apollo— still retains an aura of greatness from the days when Café Society discovered Harlem in the 1920's. It is one of the very few vaudeville theaters left in New York City. In fact, you may have to sit through some embarrassingly poor performances before you get to see any real talent —just like in the old vaudeville days.

At the eastern end of 125th Street, one arm of the Triborough Bridge reaches across to Randall's Island, one of New York City's best playgrounds with a large stadium, playing fields and picnic grounds. Most of the Puerto Rican population of New York City crosses the narrow channel separating Randall's Island from the "mainland" to celebrate the annual festival of San Juan (St. John the Baptist, patron saint of Puerto Rico) on June 24th —a tradition from their island home.

The Triborough Bridge

At Randall's Island, the Manhattan arm of the Triborough Bridge meets up with the other branch joining the Bronx and Queens. Don't miss going over this bridge, opened in 1936 and built at a cost of $60 million, one of New York City's wonders. It carries annually some 44 million vehicles (at 25c per passenger car) over its three miles of bridges and 14 miles of connecting roadways. The traffic crossing it, furthermore, is congestion-free —something close to miraculous for New York City.

The most beautiful part of uptown Manhattan lies west of Eighth Avenue along the "mountain" range that rises abruptly there and just as abruptly levels off at Riverside Drive, extending as far north as the tip of Manhattan and rising higher and higher (and becoming more beautiful) along the way until at the level of 183rd Street it reaches the dizzy height of 268 feet —about up to the Empire State Building's shinbone.

Morningside Heights

No guide book of New York City will ever neglect to mention that this section south of 125th Street, known as Morningside Heights, was the site of the revolutionary Battle of Harlem Heights —about the only skirmish that

Washington successfully waged against the British in what is now New York City. It was by no means a major military victory but after a long series of defeats in which the American revolutionary forces had to retreat from Long Island, the small military victory on Morningside Heights appeared positively gargantuan to Washington's badly demoralized troops.

St. John the Divine

At the southern end of Morningside Heights, West 110th Street passes through Frederick Douglas circle and becomes Cathedral Parkway till it ends at Riverside Drive. The name of the street was changed in honor of the Cathedral of St. John the Divine standing at Amsterdam Avenue and Cathedral Parkway. The cathedral —when completed—will be the largest Gothic church in the world. It will also be one of the most beautiful.

The cornerstone of the cathedral was laid in 1892 but it still hasn't been finished largely due to the policy of not continuing with construction until there are sufficient funds on hand to pay for it. As a result there is not one cent of debt on the building —and it still has about one third to one quarter of the way to go before it can actually claim the title of the world's largest Gothic cathedral. Nonetheless, incomplete as it is, it remains probably the most beautiful church in New York City if not in the United States. It is especially noted for the exquisiteness of its details: the tremendous bronze portals of the West Front with the beautifully carved panels depicting scenes from the Old and New Testaments; the great rose window; the richly carved Martyr's Portal of the North Tower with the sculptured figures of nine martyr-saints; the stained glass windows which, along with those of Riverside Church, are considered among the most

by TREMONT

HUDSON RIVER

HARLEM RIVER

BRONX

MARBLE HILL

INWOOD HILL PARK

W. 218TH

DYCKMAN ST.

FORT TRYON PARK

BROADWAY

TENTH AVE.

NINTH AVE.

W. 207TH

GEORGE WASHINGTON BRIDGE

W. 181ST

W. 178TH

FORT WASHINGTON

AUDUBON

BROADWAY

HIGHBRIDGE PARK

HIGH BRIDGE

W. 155TH

W. 145TH

ST. NICHOLAS AVE.

EDGECOMBE AVE.

W. 135TH

CONVENT AVE.

E. 155

W. 125TH

RIVERSIDE DRIVE

BROADWAY

AMSTERDAM AVE.

MORNINGSIDE DR.

MANHATTAN AVE.

ST. NICHOLAS AVE.

SEVENTH AVE.

LENOX AVE.

FIFTH AVE.

MADISON AVE.

PARK AVE.

LEXINGTON AVE.

THIRD AVE.

SECOND AVE.

FIRST AVE.

E. 125TH

E. 115TH

W. 118TH

CATHEDRAL PKWY.

W. 110TH

E. 110TH

PALADINO

RANDALL'S ISLAND

WARD'S ISLAND

RIVERSIDE PARK

W. END AVE.

CENTRAL PK. W.

CENTRAL PARK

FIFTH AVE.

W. 96TH

E. 96TH

outstanding of the United States; the beautiful chapels.

The most impressive and breathtaking view of the Cathedral, though, is from the gallery beneath the great rose window, where you may best appreciate the majesty of the great nave and take in almost the entire length of the church —a distance of about 601 feet, said to be the longest unbroken vista in a Christian church. Come to see the Cathedral of St. John the Divine sometime on a lovely afternoon when the sunlight streams in through the stained glass windows and paints it in lovely hues.

Columbia University

North of the Cathedral, roughly between or on 114th and 121st Streets, between Amsterdam and Claremont Avenues, cluster the 60 buildings or so making up the Morningside campus of Columbia University. It's come a long way from the day, more than 200 years ago, that it started as King's College in a vestry of Trinity Church with a total enrollment of eight students. Today Columbia University has an enrollment of more than 25,000 though less than one tenth of these are undergraduate students attending Columbia College. The remainder are enrolled in the more than 20 graduate schools which have made Columbia one of the most influential universities in the United States. Its landholdings —including the land on which stands Rockefeller Center— have also made it one of the richest.

The campus of the university is not very distinguished —how can it be, hemmed in on all sides by uninspired buildings and with not much green to relieve the general drab grayness? The Columbia group, however, is built on handsome, landscaped courts centered around the domed and classic Low Memorial Library, considered one of New York's most distinguished buildings.

Riverside Church

Northwest of Columbia University at Riverside Drive and 122nd Street stands the popular and beautiful French Gothic Riverside Church reminiscent of the famous Cathedral of Chartres in France. The stained glass windows of the Riverside Church, in fact, rank with those of the Chartres Cathedral which are considered among the finest in the world. The soaring Gothic tower of the Riverside Church, one of the most familiar "skymarks" of upper Manhattan, reaches 392 feet into the sky.

Grant National Memorial

Just northwest of Riverside Church, in splendid isolation on Riverside Park near 122nd Street, stands probably New York City's best known monument (though few New Yorkers ever go to see it): the massive and grandiose Grant's Tomb which, to everyone's great surprise, holds the remains not only of General Ulysses S. Grant but of his wife Julia Dent Grant. The monument, a neoclassic structure of gray granite, stands on a bluff 130 feet high comanding a wonderful view of the Hudson. Its interior, lined in white marble, contains besides the sarcarphogi of the Grants two trophy rooms with Civil War memorabilia as well as the bronze busts of five of the general's comrades in-arms including that of his trusted lieutenant general, William T. Sherman. Grant's Tomb (officially the General Grant National Memorial since 1958) is open (free) daily from 9 a.m. to 5 p.m.

City College

Stretching north from 130th to 140th Streets, between St. Nicholas Terrace and Amsterdam Avenue, are the 20 or so buildings —a potpourri of collegiate Gothic, neo-classic, Romanesque, renaissance, modern contem-

porary— in the main uptown campus of the City College
of the City University of New York. With an annual
enrollment of 32,000 students, City College ranks as the
largest municipal college in the world. A list of its alumni
sounds like a Who's Who in all the fields of achievements
and includes such notables as Bernard Baruch, Supreme
Court Justice Felix Frankfurter, Upton Sinclair, etc.

During the summer months hordes of music-loving
New Yorkers flock to one of City College's most popular
features —the Lewisohm Stadium where, for a nominal
fee, they can hear concerts by the New York Philharmonic
or a Metropolitan Opera Company production of Carmen
or Harry Belafonte or jazz concerts or Jascha Heifitz, etc.
The stadium seats 18,000 and performers often play to
a capacity audience. For a schedule of the programs being
presented at Lewisohm Stadium (but only during the
summer), consult the daily papers or call AD 4-5800.

Continue your northward march up wayward Broadway. You'll eventually come upon Trinity Cemetery,
quietly spreading from 153rd to 155th Street on either
side of the avenue, the largest graveyard in Manhattan
which began as an overflow from crowded Trinity Churchyard in New York's financial district. This Trinity Cemetery holds, among others, the 700 displaced graves from
St. Luke's in Greenwich Village —including that of
Clement C. Moore. On the tombstones are such august
names as Astor, Schermerhorn, Havemeyer, etc. Also rest-
ing here is the great naturalist and artist, John James
Audubon, who once had a farm in these parts.

The Museum Group

Across the way from the cemetery, grouped around
a striking plaza (Audubon Terrace, once the home of
Audubon) are five museums whose existence most New

Yorkers ignore. The museums must be entered through the court and are thus set apart from the thoroughfare and go unnoticed by the average passerby. Don't miss them. Two of the museums are unique. The buildings clustered around the handsome plaza are:

- **The American Academy of Arts & Letters**

As its name implies, it is a society of august personages from American arts and letters but occasionally —generally from May through June— the society exhibits works (including paintings, sculptures, books, manuscripts, etc.) by newly elected members. Also, from time to time during fall and winter, there are special exhibits. The Academy is open (admission free) daily except Mondays during the exhibitions from 2 to 5 p.m.

- **The American Geographical Society of New York**

It has an excellent collection of maps and other geographical material in its reference library. It, too, is open to the public weekdays from 9 a.m. to 4:45 p.m. It is closed weekends and holidays.

- **The American Numismatic Society**

This society has the first and only-one-of-its-kind collection devoted entirely to numismatics —the study of coins, tokens, medals, paper money. It has a particularly fine collection of ancient Greek, Roman and Far Eastern coins. One exhibit traces the development of coins from their beginning 2600 years ago to the present; another does the same with medals. Exhibits are open Tuesdays through Saturdays from 10 a.m. to 5 p.m. The society also maintains the most comprehensive numismatic library in the United States and it is open to the public (for reference) Tuesdays through Saturdays from 9 a.m. to 5 p.m. Both exhibits and library are closed weekends and holidays. Admission to either is free.

- **The Hispanic Society of America**

The society maintains a collection of paintings, sculptures and examples of the decorative arts by exclusively Hispanic artists dating from prehistoric times to the present. Among the painters represented are Morales, El Greco, Ribera, Velázquez, Goya, Zuloaga. The library collection is particularly fine and includes among its 10,000 early imprints, the sole remaining leaf of the first Bible to be issued in the vernacular (the Valencian Bible). Admission to both library and museum is free. The museum is open Tuesdays through Saturdays from 10 a.m. to 4:30 p.m., Sundays from 2 to 5 p.m. The library is open Tuesdays through Saturdays from 1 to 4:30 p.m. It is closed Sundays, Mondays and all major holidays.

- **Museum of the American Indian (Heye Foundation)**

This is the world's largest Indian museum, housing a unique collection of the art and artifacts not only of the Indians of the United States, but of all the Americas. You'll be interested in seeing the masks of the Iroquois False Face Society and the work of the Central and South American Indians. Youngsters will get a thrill out of seeing some of the personal possessions of such familiar figures as Red Cloud, Sitting Bull, Arapoosch, etc. The museum is open (free) Tuesdays through Sundays from 1 to 5 p.m. and is closed all Mondays and holidays.

East of the museum group, at St. Nicholas Avenue and 155th Street, stands the Polo Grounds, its 60,000 seats desolately empty most of the year. At one time the swells used to make the journey this far north to watch —and play— polo. Later it became the home of the New York Giants who eventually deserted it for the greener grass in San Francisco (and were thus reunited with their great rivals, the Brooklyn Dodgers, who themselves had deserted Ebbets Field for Los Angeles). For a brief spell the Polo Grounds was home for the losing (but loved) Mets who are now quite happy with their new quarters —the William Shea Stadium in Flushing, Queens.

Jumel Mansion

Just northwest of the Polo Grounds, from its hilly site at Edgecombe Avenue and 160th Street, the Jumel Mansion looks down in elegant aloofness at "Sugar Hill" —one of Harlem's most elite residential sections. One of the few really elegant colonial homes left standing in New York City, the Jumel Mansion was built originally in 1765 for Roger Morris and family who left Manhattan rather hurriedly when trouble developed between Mother England and her American children. Washington, much obliged, used the house as headquarters for a brief spell before he was forced to retreat from Manhattan. The conquering British appreciated elegance, too, and used it as a headquarters for seven long years. Finally Stephan Jumel, a wealthy French merchant, on the instigation of his wife, Eliza, bought and made the mansion his home. When Mons. Jumel died he left his wealth and the lovely house to his wife thus making her, it was said, the richest woman in the United States. Mme. Jumel, a rather extraordinary woman, at the age of 60 subsequently married the equally extraordinary Aaron Burr who though 78 was apparently still active. The Jumel-Burrs soon separated. Aaron Burr died shortly after but his estranged widow lived another score and ten before she was finally and irrevocably parted from her mansion. Eventually, the city bought the property and converted it into the lovely historical museum it is today. The Georgian-colonial style house is furnished as it must have been in the days of the Morrises, the Jumels and the Burrs. It is open Tuesdays through Sundays from 11 a.m. to 5 p.m. admission free.

High Bridge

To the southeast of the Jumel Mansion starts the thin slither of green that further north widens slightly into narrow High Bridge Park. At the level of 174th Street —it can be reached from 173rd Street by foot— soars the striking, more-than-a-century old High Bridge, a Roman-style aqueduct built as part of the Croton water system (completed in 1848) and still carrying water. Though it has since been partly rebuilt to improve navigation through the narrow channel of the Harlem River, some of its huge original stone arches remain. It is an imposing sight seen from the Harlem River Drive. A foot path permits pedestrian traffic across the bridge and if you're not adverse to heights, the view is worth the walk.

George Washington Bridge

Northwest of High Bridge, connecting upper Manhattan to Fort Lee in New Jersey, soars another engineering marvel —the beautiful George Washington Bridge, the only 14-lane, two-level suspension bridge and the third longest suspension bridge in the world. (It lost the title of first to the San Francisco Golden Gate, recently surpassed by the as yet not completed Verrazano-Narrows Bridge.) More than 100,000 miles of wire (in the main cables) suspend the 4,760-foot span. The Port of New York Authority to date has sunk over $221 million into the George Washington Bridge which presently carries some 44 million vehicles annually.

A few blocks north of the George Washington Bridge, at 701 Fort Washington Avenue, is the Mother Cabrini High School where, in the chapel in a glass sepulchre, is enshrined the body of Mother Cabrini (St. Frances Xavier Cabrini), the first American to be canonized by the Roman Catholic Church.

The George Washington Bridge

The Cloisters

As you proceed north along the slender index finger of Manhattan Island pointing to the western section of the Bronx, the terrain becomes more rugged and more beautiful. Starting at the level of 190th Street and extending north to the level of 203rd Street is what has been called America's most beautiful park —the small, jewel-like Fort Tyron Park, rising in a series of terraces, rock gardens and woody green slopes from the Hudson River to a ridge bounded on the east by Broadway. At its crest, a circular lookout, with a flag pole marking the spot where once stood Fort Tyron (held briefly by Washington's forces), affords an incomparable view of the Hudson, the Jersey Palisades and the graceful George Washington Bridge. The city spreading to the south seems very far away —almost in another age.

In a world apart, too, its tower rising above the green trees in the northern edge of the park, is the museum of medieval art known as the Cloisters. The park, the Cloisters and most of the museum's collection were donated by John D. Rockefeller, Jr. who, to complete his masterpiece of munificence, bought about 13 miles of land north of the George Washington Bridge in New Jersey and gave it to the Palisades Interstate Park Commission just to be sure that no one would ever spoil the near perfect view from the Cloisters.

The museum building itself, a remarkable and wondrously harmonious blending of sections from several medieval structures, was imported stone by stone from Europe. It consists of the cloisters from five medieval monasteries (hence its name), a Romanesque chapel and a 12th century chapter house and Spanish apse. Its collection includes the famous Unicorn Tapestries (depicting the allegorical "Hunt of the Unicorn") which rank as one of the world's greatest art treasures. Not to be missed either are the Chalice of Antioch, the earliest known Christian chalice; the two Book of Hours, beautifully illuminated.

Most visitors will agree that the Cloisters is literally "out of this world" —the peace and serenity, the incomparable setting and medieval atmosphere give one the feeling of being in a world very far removed from atom bombs and space capsules. Most visitors will also agree

The Cloisters

that it is the most beautiful museum they've ever visited.

The Cloisters is open Tuesdays through Saturdays from 10 a.m. to 5 p.m., Sundays and holidays from 1 to 5 p.m. (from May to September until 6 p.m.).

Bounding the Cloisters on the north runs Dykeman Street, a ravine that separates Fort Tyron Park from its wild and woolly neighbor to the north, Inwood Hill Park. The street is named after a wealthy Dutch family who once upon a time held claim to most of rugged northern Manhattan. Their residence, built around 1783, still stands —almost unnoticed— wedged in by its neighbors at 204th Street and Broadway. It's the only early Dutch farmhouse left standing on Manhattan and the city now maintains it —authentically furnished as it was in the days of the

Knickerbockers, complete to old Dutch oven and charming Dutch garden— as a museum, opened from 10 a.m. to 5 p.m. Tuesdays through Sundays, admission free.

Inwood Hill Park

To the north of Dykeman Street spreads triangular Inwood Hill Park, the only section of primitivism left on sophisticated Manhattan, an untouched wilderness much as it was on the day that Henry Hudson first sighted New York harbor —though 3½ centuries older. Some of the park's giant trees were giants at the time and the centuries haven't diminished them. On the northern edge of Inwood Hill, on a spot known as Spuyten Duyvil, once stood the Indian settlement of *Shorakapkok* ("as far as the sitting down place") and Indian remains —weapons, utensils —have been found there. Though today the Indians are gone, the rugged terrain and the wonderful view of the Hudson and Harlem Rivers remain and it's not difficult to imagine yourself as far away from Manhattan as 3½ centuries ago.

But the story of Manhattan doesn't end here at Spuyten Duyvil. Beyond the river is a spot called Marble Hill —it used to have marble quarries— whose residents probably feel that, figuratively speaking, they are neither fish nor fowl. Years ago, when the Harlem River was rerouted to allow barges to pass from the East to the Hudson River, Marble Hill was physically separated from Manhattan and, geographically, became a part of the Bronx. Down in the municipal books, though, Marble Hill remains —legally and politically— a part of Manhattan and its only natural (though schizophrenic) connection with the American mainland. Perhaps that's why New York City (Manhattan) is like no other city in the United States —or in the world for that matter.

10

Bronck's Land
and the 'Out Islands'

Now that you've explored Manhattan's 22.6 square miles, you only have the other 297 square miles of the four remaining boroughs to go. Don't panic. This acreage is in large part residential in character and has comparatively few —and widely scattered— points of interest. Most of your traveling now will be done by subway.

The Bronx

First on the itinerary is the Bronx —originally Bronck's Land when it was first settled in 1641— spreading to the north of Manhattan and Queens, the only one of the five boroughs to be solidly on Mainland, U.S.A.

Certainly, no visit to New York City could be complete without at least one visit to Bronx Park with its justly famous botanical garden and zoological park.

■ New York Botanical Garden

The New York Botanical Garden —230 acres covered with 12,000 plant varieties— always has some display to make you hold your breath no matter what time of the year you visit it: Spring for the magnolias, dogwoods, Japanese cherry trees, tulips, hyacinths, etc.; in summer bloom the lilac, the peonies and, of course, the roses; in fall the chrysanthemums and the flaming autumn leaves; in winter and all year long the lush foliage and exotic blooms of the Garden's 11 greenhouses —one entire acre under glass. The Garden is open every day from 10 a.m. to half an hour after sunset and admission is free. To get to the Garden take the New York Central Harlem Division at Grand Central Station to the Botanical Garden Station. By subway, take the IND-Sixth Avenue "D" train (Concourse-205th Street) to Bedford Park Boulevard; or the IRT-Seventh Avenue to 149th Street station. Here change for the Third Avenue El and get off at 200th Street.

■ **New York Zoological Park**

The real star attraction of Bronx Park is the New York Zoological Park, better known as the Bronx Zoo, one of the largest (only London's is larger) and most unique in the world. More than 2½ million people come to visit its nearly 3,000 animal specimens annually —a record attendance for a zoo— and there must be a reason for this mass invasion of such a "remote" area as the Bronx. There is —the zoo's display techniques. For example, there's the part where the animals are allowed to roam freely over an "African veldt" —at least, the closest thing to it outside Africa— isolated from visitors by a moat; the "Jewel Room" where the visitor is left in the dark but where brilliantly feathered friends from the tropics are brightly illuminated; the habitat cages where birds live amid real plants and foliage; the reptile house with the world's largest collection of reptiles.

To get to the Bronx Zoo, take any IRT subway —the East 180th Street Express or the White Plains Road Express—to 177th Street. The Zoo is open all year round from 10 a.m. to at least 4:30 p.m. (sometimes later depending upon the season). Admission is free except Tuesdays, Wednesdays & Thursdays (but not if a holiday) when admission is 25c for anyone five years or older.

Especially charming is the Zoo's famed Children's Zoo where the youngsters may pet and feed all sorts of petable and feedable animals. This miniature zoo is open from Easter to mid-November (in good weather only) from 10:30 a.m. to half an hour before the main zoo's closing time. Admission is 25c for children from 1 to 14 years; anyone else, 20c. Adults must bring a child.

■ Freedomland

For the children, a trip to New York City cannot be complete without a visit to Freedomland —though this is likely to cost the parents a small fortune. Essentially, Freedomland is a large amusement park, shaped like the United States, where each diversion is supposed to present some event or facet of American history. For example, there's a "Little Old New York" setting with policemen in bobby hats and long coats ready to give you directions and answer other questions; there's an every-20-minute re-enactment of the Chicago fire complete with Mrs. O'Leary's cow, real flames and an old-fashioned Chicago fire department to put out the conflagration; there's a western gun duel with a good guy, a bad guy, etc.

Freedomland is open daily from Memorial Day to Labor Day from 10 a.m. to 11 p.m.; after that only on weekends. Admission is $1.00 for adults; 75c for children from 12 to 17; 50c for children under 12. The only trouble is that once inside Freedomland some of the special exhibits also charge admission. By the end of the day your wallet is liable to be considerably leaner than what it was in the morning. Nonetheless, the children will be absolutely enchanted and —provided you have the where-withal— the look on their faces will be worth any price.

To get to Freedomland (Baychester and Bartow Avenues), take the IRT-Seventh Avenue-Dyre Avenue line to the Gun Hill Road Station or the IRT-Lexington Avenue line to Pelham Bay Park Station. Shuttle buses at both stations go directly to the amusement park.

■ Other Parks

Two other parks in the Bronx have special attractions: Van Cortland Park (with the usual park facilities) has the Van Cortland House Museum (Broadway and 242nd Street), a colonial farmhouse built in 1748 and now maintained as a museum by the National Society of Colonial Dames of New York. It is open daily (except Mondays) from 10 a.m. to 5 p.m.; Sundays from 2 to 5 p.m. Admission is free on Fridays and Saturdays only; 25c all other days. To get there take the IRT-Broadway line to the 242nd Street-Van Cortland Park Station (the last stop).

Pelham Bay Park with the Bronx's largest (and most crowded) public beach —Orchard— has another historic house, the *Bartow Mansion,* built in 1836-42 and furnished in the 19th century style, with a magnificent sunken garden built by the International Garden Club who use the mansion as headquarters. It is open to the public Tuesdays, Fridays and Sundays from 1 to 5 p.m. and admission is 25c. Children under 12 must be accompanied by an adult but they are admitted free. The mansion is on Shore Road just east of the Hutchinson River Parkway at Pelham Bay Park.

Brooklyn

The second oldest (first settled in 1636 as Breuckelen) and second largest borough, Brooklyn is more a state of mind than a geographic division of New York City. Its 3 million inhabitants —it is also the most populated borough— consider themselves first and foremost (and almost to the exclusion of everything else) Brooklynites, never New Yorkers.

■ Coney Island

Brooklyn has several outstanding attractions but by far the most popular is *Coney Island* —so named for the *Konijn* (Dutch for rabbits) that overran it. The rabbits have long since been frightened off —probably by the annual mass invasion of some 45 million sweating human bodies looking for a place in the sun and the surf. Coney Island combines a wonderful beach (but only at its best in uncrowded winter) and boardwalk with a perpetual carnival in full swing —the greatest collection of amusement rides and other diversions to be found anywhere in the world. (Too great, too wearing —for some.) Nonetheless, despite the moist mobs and the honky tonk and the hucksters, no child or teenager should be deprived of the thrill of riding the Cyclone or Thunderbolt (the kings of the roller-coasters) at least once. (If you have a weak heart, don't try it and by no means take the little ones on it. There are plenty of other less heart-taxing rides.)

Prices for the rides at Coney Island range from 10c to 50c. You may buy a book of tickets of 15 punches (the equivalent of 1.50) for $1.00; 30 punches for $1.50. To get there take any train of the BMT line or the IND "D" train to the last stop (Stillwell Avenue-Coney Island).

■ New York Aquarium

Next to Coney Island's honky-tonk splashes one of Brooklyn's (and New York City's) top attractions —the New York Aquarium with its wonderful collection of mustachioed walruses and sea lions, its dangerously lazy-looking sharks, its elegant penguins, its brilliant tropical fish and coral reefs and a host of other fishy odds and ends found round and about New York's waters. Star feature is an electrifying performance by the Aquarium's electric eel which, every hour on the hour, after some coaxing —i.e., tickling— discharges 650 volts.

You may get to the Aquarium by taking the IND "D" train or the BMT-Brighton local to West 8th Street at Coney Island or by taking the BMT-Sea Beach or West End to Stillwell Avenue and there taking the IND or Brighton local to West 8th Street. Admission is 90c for adults, 45c for children from 5 to 16.

■ Prospect Park and the Botanical Garden

One of Brooklyn's most beautiful features is Prospect Park which, outside of Fort Tyron Park, is considered by many to be New York City's loveliest. It, too, was designed by Olmsted who gave it an especially wild beauty making it seem twice the size of its 526 acres. However, for all its "wildness," it has the usual recreational facilities plus a comparatively small but fine zoo and an old Dutch Colonial farmhouse built in 1770 —the Lefferts Homestead— and maintained by the Department of Parks as a Revolutionary museum with furnishings of the period. It's open Mondays, Wednesdays and Fridays from 1 to 5 p.m., admission free.

Across the way from the park blooms the Brooklyn Botanical Garden. Though it is considerably smaller than the New York Botanical Gardens —a mere 50 acres— it receives more than half again as many visitors annually as the latter. Perhaps the principal reason for this is that everyone flocks to see (in late April and early May) the blossoming of the Japanese cherry trees —probably New York City's most exquisite sight. Also outstanding: the enchanting dream-like Japanese Garden and a unique Garden of Fragrance for the blind. The Botanical Garden is open daily from 8:30 a.m. (Sundays and holidays from 10 a.m.) to half an hour before sunset. Admission is free. To get there take the BMT-Brighton express to the Prospect Park Station or the IRT-Seventh Avenue to the Eastern Parkway-Brooklyn Museum Station.

■ Brooklyn Museum

Another outstanding point of interest in Brooklyn stands right next door to the Brooklyn Botanical Garden: the Brooklyn Museum, one of the seven major art museums in the United States. Its Department of Ancient Egyptian Art, in fact, has the largest collection of Egyptian art in the Western Hemisphere and its Egyptological Library is one of the world's most important.

The museum is open daily (except Christmas) from 10 a.m. to 5 p.m. weekdays and from 1 to 5 p.m. Sundays and holidays. Admission is free. To get there take the IRT-Broadway train to the Brooklyn Museum station.

Staten Island and Queens

Normally, few visitors ever get to see New York's two remaining boroughs —Staten Island and Queens— though together they make up more than 50% of the city's land area. The average New York, in fact, knows nothing about Staten Island except that it is on the other side of the Staten Island ferryboat ride —a trip he occasionally takes for the joy of it. He may know a little more about Queens because every now and then he has call to use or welcome visitors at one of its two airports (LaGuardia and the John F. Kennedy International Airport), but more likely because he hopes to make some money at New York's only two thoroughbred race tracks —the famous and classic Belmont Race Track (opened in 1905), which New Yorkers consider their very own though it lies just east of Queens limits, and the "new" Aqueduct Race Track, renovated in 1959 at a cost of $33 million. Most likely, though, the average New Yorker gets to "see" Queens on the way to visiting relatives or beaches (especially Jones Beach) "out on the island."

This lack of interest in more than 50% of New York City is quite understandable. Staten Island —or, more technically, Richmond— is, in comparison to Manhattan, incredibly bucolic, sprinkled with little hamlets nestled among rolling hills. (It, by the way, can boast of having the highest point on the Atlantic Coast from Florida to Maine —Todt Hill— reaching the dizzy height of 431 feet.) A good deal of Staten Island's rusticity is attributable to its complete isolation from the other islands, its only connection (for the present) with the rest of New York City being the Staten Island Ferry. Staten Island's peace and quiet is scheduled to be shattered in 1965 with the completion of the Verrazano-Narrows Bridge joining it to Brooklyn. Meanwhile, its chief points of interest are: a zoo —the **Barrett Zoo**— with a surprisingly good reptile house —should you go in for reptiles; the **Vorrlezer House,** built prior to 1696, the oldest known schoolhouse still standing in the United States; a couple of museums concentrating mostly on Staten Island history and features; the especially noteworthy **Jacques Marchais Center of Tibetan Art** —a museum in the form of a Tibetan temple with beautiful gardens, a fine collection of Tibetan Buddhist art, an excellent library on oriental countries —and, unfortunately, most inconvenient and spotty hours. Phone (EL 1-3280) before going.

Like Staten Island, Queens, too —the largest of the boroughs— is mostly a residential area and normally, outside of the race tracks and airports mentioned, has little to attract the visitor. For the next two years, however, in its Flushing Meadow Park, it will hold New York City's greatest drawing card —the fabulous 1964-1965 New York World's Fair— deserving a chapter all to itself.

11 | *The Fair of Fairs*

Any excuse is a good excuse to have a party and the 300th anniversary of New York City appeared to the City Fathers to be better than most. So they took up the matter with the Powers-That-Were in Washington (at that time, President Dwight D. Eisenhower). From this little acorn was nurtured the 646 fabulous acres in Flushing Meadow Park (Queens) which, during their two-year tenure, are expected to delight, entertain and amaze a conservatively estimated 70 million visitors. If these expectations are realized, the 1964-1965 New York World's Fair will have had the greatest attendance in the history of international expositions.

The British started the trend back in 1851 when Queen Victoria's Prince Albert sired the first "International Exposition" held in the "Crystal Palace" constructed for just that purpose. The world's first world's fair was a social and sterling success. With the ice broken —and with such a profitable example at that— the world broke out into such a rash of world's fairs that the Bureau of International Expositions was formed to lower a modest shade on the mass exhibitionism. Under the rules of the BIE, no member nation can participate in more than one world's fair per hemisphere per decade.

Though the Seattle World's Fair only folded its tents in October of 1962, nothing daunted, the indefatigable ex-Parks Commissioner Robert Moses, president of the New York World's Fair 1964-1965 Corporation —with an occasional assist by a staff of hundreds— has managed to put together a world's fair that will be hard to duplicate in this century much less in the next ten years, though BIE rules were to permit. It hasn't been easy. At one point, Robert Moses, a man who has acquired an almost international fame for his pithy epistles, obviously entangled (and exasperated) by governmental red tape —and patently wishing the gods had made it otherwise— wrote:

> "As to other delays, it is to be remembered that the States require both executive and legislative action, that City contracts must be carried out under charter requirements, and that foreign nations cannot be ordered about or unduly pressured."

Nonetheless, despite the delays and setbacks, the disappointments and frustrations, Fair President Moses has all along kept predicting to the pessimists and armchair generals that out of the early chaos at Flushing Meadow was going to emerge on April 22nd, 1964 a Fair fabulous in every respect —in entertainment, in attendance, financially. According to the latest available figures, the Fair Corporation expects to gross some $158,450,000 through ticket sales, space rentals and other odds and ends. After the Fair closes and the last free-form pavilion is, alas, demolished or carted away, the Corporation, a non-profit organization which cannot line its own pockets, expects to be able to return to New York City the $24 million it advanced for certain park improvements and an additional $26 million slated for educational purposes and other park improvements. If the Fair Corporation realizes its financial projections —and all advanced signs seem to indicate that it will— the 1964-1965 New York World's Fair will join the handful to have been profitable —and the only one in New York City's history to have even paid its way. In any case, New York City will be left with several widened and extended highways, a new stadium and botanical gardens, an enlarged marina and amphitheater, a permanent and imposing Hall of Science, a New York Port of Authority heliport, a much improved Flushing Meadow Park —and millions of New Yorkers and visitors will be left with hundreds of exciting memories.

If there had to be an excuse for the Fair, there also had to be an ideal to give it purpose and a theme to give it unity. The Fair's purpose —"Peace through Understanding"— certainly expresses a hope that knows no territorial limits. The Fair's theme —"Man's Achievements in an Expanding Universe"— has resulted in one of the greatest and most fascinating expositions of men's handiwork ever gathered together for one purpose. Because it is impossible to tell you of all the wonders that you'll see within the boundaries of those fabulous 646 acres at Flushing Meadow Park, only the main highlights of the Fair will be described. However, before you step past the tall, distinctive entrance towers opening onto this fascinating world of achievements, you'll want to know a few preliminary facts.

Traveling to the Fair

The 1964-1965 World's Fair stands precisely in the geographical center of Metropolitan New York, in Flushing Meadow Park (Queens), where the 1939-1940 World's Fair made history —though no profits. How do you get there? It's simple. The wily Fair planners have done everything to facilitate a mass influx of callers at the Fair gates. They can come by land, by sea, by air or underground.

Via Subway: The underground method is certainly the least expensive and one of the simplest. A 15c subway token —and a series of blue markers— will take you from any point in New York City to the main entrance of the Fair via one or a combination of the city's three subway systems —IRT, BMT or IND. Eventually you'll find yourself on the IRT-Flushing Line headed towards the reconstructed and modernized Willets Point Boulevard Station where a newly constructed overpass will lead you directly to the Fair's main entrance. The New York Transit Authority ordered $50 million worth of air conditioned subway cars —designed by Raymond Loewy no less— for the shuttle run between Grand Central Station and the Fair. This subway system can carry up to 150,000 persons per day.

Traveling time from Grand Central Station to the Willets Point Boulevard Station: approximately 20 minutes.

Via Rail: The Long Island Rail Road will take you via special express trains leaving Pennsylvania Station (in Manhattan) directly to the specially constructed World's Fair Station in front of the main entrance. Those coming from Long Island may take a special express train from Jamaica Station to the Fair, or the Port Washington Branch trains which serve the Fair directly.

Fare from Penn Station to the Fair is 50c each way. (Children under five may ride free.) However, you can save as much as $1.00 on some round trip fares if you buy a combination round trip-World's Fair admission ticket. For example, the special combination price from New York City is $2.50, a savings of 50c; from Freeport, Long Island, $3.15, a savings of $1.00. If you're traveling in a group of 30 or more, you can save even more.

Via Bus: Many New York City and Long Island bus companies are providing service to the Fair. Rates, vary, naturally according to the departure points. The Grey Line Corporation, for example, charges $1.00 from midtown Manhattan to the Fair.

Via Car: Construction improvement programs on the major approaches to the Fair —as Long Island-New York City commuters, slowed down to a crawl, know only too well— were started several years prior to the opening of the Fair. Some $125 million (and many times that number of cuss words) later, an improved Grand Central Parkway, Whitestone Expressway, Northern Boulevard and Van Wyck Expressway and the other major approaches, with trail blazer markings pointing the way, are providing rapid access to the Fair. Three major expressways touch the Fairgrounds directly: the Grand Central Parkway passing right through the width of the Fairgrounds and separating the Transportation Area from the Federal and State Area on the west; the Van Wyck Expressway skirting the Industrial Area on the east; and the Long Island Expressway separating the Lake Amusement Area from the Federal-State and International Areas.

If you're coming from midtown Manhattan, the Midtown Tunnel and Long Island Expressway is the most direct approach. Uptowners and those in the western part of the Bronx will want to cross over by way of the Triborough Bridge and take the Grand Central Parkway. Eastern Bronxites will find the Bronx-Whitestone Bridge, the Whitestone Expressway and the Van Wyck Expressway the best route. Those really far east may prefer the Throgs Neck bridge to the Cross Island Parkway (heading west) to the Whitestone Parkway and from thence to the Van Wyck Expressway.

Eastern Long Islanders may use any of their preferred major arteries heading towards the city to get them to the Van Wyck Expressway or the Long Island Expressway. Those in South Brooklyn should take the Belt Parkway to the Van Wyck Expressway, while those in the north of the borough will find the Brooklyn Queens Expressway to the Long Island Expressway best.

Parking facilities in the immediate Fairground vicinity

can accommodate some 25,000 cars (at $1.50 per day) with free bus shuttle service to the admission gates. Parking at nearby Flushing Airport, however, is 75c per day with an additional 15c charge for shuttle service.

By Sea: If you want to try your sea legs, come to the Fair by boat. The newly enlarged and modernized World's Fair Marina in Flushing Bay, occupying 240 acres of sea and land, can accommodate some 1000 boats, with the possibility of expanding to accommodate an additional 1000 if need be. The Marina Complex —the world's largest floating Marina— consists of seven circular islands of Fiberglas connected by a network of floating finger piers and provides a full range of boating services (marine supplies, storage for gear, fuel, etc.) plus such landlubber luxuries as a cocktail lounge and restaurant, TV, dressing rooms, laundromats, etc. At night, the translucent colored Fiberglas centers, lit from within, act as beacon lights for homeward bound skippers. After the Fair, the Marina will continue to serve boat owners in the Flushing Bay area. You can sail to the Marina via the Intracoastal Waterway, the Hudson River and the New York State Barge Canal.

Rates for docking at the Marina are the following: *Seasonal* (April 1 through October 31st) for a slip — $13.00 per foot of finger pier or boat, whichever is greater; for a mooring — $5.40 per foot. *Monthly:* slip — $5.40 per foot; mooring — $2.70 per foot. *Overnight (24 hours):* slip — 20c per foot; mooring — 10c per foot. There is an additional charge for electricity and water.

For those who like the water route, but not under their own steam, there are guided Circle Line cruises leaving from midtown Manhattan which sail around lower Manhattan, give you a glimpse of the Statue of Liberty and then up the East River to Flushing Bay and the World's Fair Marina. Fare: $2.75 for adults; $1.25 for children under 12. Return fare which must be bought at the Fairgrounds is $2.00 and $1.00 respectively. Boats leave at 10 a.m. and 2 p.m.; return at 11:45 p.m. and 4 p.m.

By Air: All roads lead to New York and all major (as well as most minor) airlines land at New York's "new" LaGuardia Airport, the fabulous John F. Kennedy Airport (formerly New York International Airport; more commonly, Idlewild) and New Jersey's Newark Airport. Most airlines are offering special package deals which combine transportation with a tour of the City as well as a visit (or several visits) to the Fair. As a matter of fact, the variety offered by the airlines (and travel agencies) is limited only by your budget and your imagination.

If you're the kind that can't wait to touch ground to see the Fair, New York Airways will provide you with helicopter service from all three airports to the New York Port of Authority heliport at the Fair. The same company also has 30 flights leaving daily between 9 a.m. and midnight from the heliport atop the Pan Am Building in the heart of Manhattan to the Fair's heliport —and providing camera fans with spectacular views of both Manhattan and the Fair. Rates: $9.00 per person. Children under two fly free of charge.

One airline (Eastern) provides direct bus-shuttle service for its customers from the airport to its terminal at the Fair for the regular price of admission to the Fair.

Cost of Admission to Fair

■ *Individual Tickets:* adults — $2.00; children under 13 years — $1.00; children under two admitted free.

■ *Twenty-Ticket Book:* adults — $30.00; children — $15.00.

Rates are for the 1964 season only. Tickets bought during 1964, however, are valid for 1965.

■ *School children:* After some verbal fights between the Roberts —Robert Wagner, who is determined to see that his future constituents are treated well, and Robert Moses, who is determined to see that the Fair shows a profit— it was decided that school children, accompanied by their teacher during school hours, would be admitted to the Fair for 25c.

When to Come to the Fair

Come to the Fair anytime between 9:30 a.m. and 2 a.m. —most exhibits are open between 10 a.m. and 10 p.m., but some (especially those featuring entertainment) are open until the wee hours— starting with Wednesday, April 22nd, 1964 until October 18th, 1964 when the Fair will temporarily lock its gates and hibernate till spring. On Wednesday, April 21st, 1965, the Fair will once again be open for business until October 17th, 1965 when it will close its gates on the heels of its last visitor.

Getting Around at the Fair

As with the 1939-1940 World's Fair, transportation at the Fairgrounds —other than your own two feet— is officially in the hands of Greyhound at the World's Fair, Inc. Greyhound offers you the following services:

▪ Free transportation between the Fair parking lots bordering Meadow Lake and the admission gates.

▪ A quick way of getting from one widely separated point to another via rapid, air conditioned buses traveling along the road circling the Fair. These buses stop at all eight admission gates as well as 27 intermediate, sheltered stations equipped with directional data and maps of the Fairgrounds.

Fare: 25c (for a ride covering the entire perimeter of the Fairgrounds or any part thereof).

▪ A **"Grand Tour"** of the grounds via air conditioned, glass-domed buses. The electronically lectured tour lasts about 1½ hours and passes all the major exhibits located on the 8 miles of roadway open to bus travel. Fair-goers may board at stations adjacent to all eight admission gates.

Fare: adults — $3.00; children under 12 — $1.50; children under 2 ride free.

▪ An **"Escorter"** service providing a "where-you-want-to-go" guided tour in an open, four-passenger vehicle with driver-guide covering roadways and walkways not open to other forms of mechanized transportation.

Fare: $9.00 per hour for two passengers plus $1.00 for

each additional passenger up to four. Minimum charge is $3.00 for two passengers for 20 minutes.

■ A **"Glide-a-Ride"** service providing local transportation between east and west and north and south extremeties via a 60-passenger, open-air, tractor train.

Fare: 25c for a ride going from one extremity to the other or any stop along the direction of travel.

■ *"Glide-a-Ride"* lectured tours of three different areas of the Fair lasting from half an hour to 45 minutes.

Fare: For Area Tour "A" passing through the International Area, circling the Lake Amusement Area and skirting the Industrial Area — $1.00 for adults, 50c for children under 12; for Area Tour "B" (primarily of the Industrial Area) — 75c for adults, 50c for children under 12; for Area Tour "C" (primarily of the Transportation Area but passing through part of the Federal and State Area) — 75c for adults, 50c for children under 12.

Information at the Fair

One of the best ways to become orientated at the Fair is to stop by the American Express Pavilion near the main entrance. Focal point of the exhibit is the official scale model of the Fairgrounds with all the pavilions, avenues and routes of access to the Fair faithfully laid out. A five-minute, taped "briefing," dramatically presented through an artful combination of light and sound, describes the Fair and its main attractions.

As previously mentioned, maps and other directional information are also available at the sheltered Greyhound bus stations along the Fairgrounds' perimeter roadway. However, for answers to more specific questions —such as the time and place for special events— try any one of the 20 or so Official World's Fair Information Booths where there will be uniformed Greyhound attendants waiting to answer your questions. These booths are connected by phone and teletype to the Official World's Fair Information Center and thus have the latest word (officially, that is) on Fair doings. Language, furthermore, should be no barrier for many of the operators at the telephone information center were chosen for their proficiency in many languages.

In addition, electronic bulletins at the dozen or so General Foods Information Arches, located at key sites throughout the Fairgrounds, will flash the latest Fair news and information on special events.

Rest and Refuge

Neither the Fair planners nor the exhibitors have neglected the physical necessities of Fair visitors. The Fair people have provided restrooms with uniformed attendants at strategically (and widely) distributed areas throughout the Fairgrounds. Exhibitors also have lavatory facilities for visitors as well as personnel. One —the Scott Paper Company— bills its restroom facilities as "the most luxurious at the Fair" and provides a special diaper-changing room for mothers with as yet undomesticated babies.

For those suffering from Fair fatigue, those thoughtful planners have very kindly provided contour-shaped Fiberglas benches along the landscaped avenues, boulevard and promenades of the Fairgrounds, and hardly an exhibitor has failed to include at least a few scattered benches on the exhibit site. The following, however, are offering really secluded oasis of quiet amidst the hurly-burly of the Fair: the Dynamic Maturity Pavilion in the Industrial Area and the Christian Science, the Church of Jesus Christ of the Latter Day Saints, the Garden of Meditation, the Billy Graham, the Protestant and Orthodox Center and the Vatican Pavilions, all in the International Area.

If, however, your weary bones yearn for something more soft and restful than a park or chapel bench or chair, hie yourself over to the Simmons "Land of Enchantment Beautyrest Center" in the Industrial Area. The two top floors of this restful pavilion are turned over to 46 rentable roomettes with soothing decor and Simmons beds with disposable sheets. A Simmons "Beautyrest Lady" is on hand to escort you to your slumber haven —and escort you out again (forcibly, if necessary) when your allowable half hour catnap is up. Charge to the weary is $1.00.

Restaurants

If nothing else, the Fair's planners and exhibitors have made sure of one thing: no visitor will starve for want of a place to eat. Some 90 restaurants and snack bars scattered throughout the Fairgrounds (the largest number in the International Area) provide a total seating capacity for approximately 20,000 diners and offer anything from the budget-priced menus of the 25 refreshment centers operated by The Brass Rail, the foot long hot dogs at the Century Grill, the 99c seven-course dinners at the Chun King Corporation tea houses and Riksha Inn to the ultimate in luxury and exotic fare of the international restaurants.

Other Facilities at the Fair

■ Even the physically handicapped, the infirm and the toddlers have had someone to cater to their interests. Equipment for Fairs, Inc. rents wheelchairs for adults at $4.50 per day, and strollers for children up to 7 or 8 years of age at $2.00 per day.

■ RCA is also rendering the greatest service at the Fair to anguished parents by acting as the Found Department for the lost. At regular intervals weeping progeny are paraded in front of the color TV cameras so that misplaced parents can reclaim their own by watching for them on the more than 230 color TV sets scattered throughout the Fairgrounds.

■ Finally, if you're in need of banking services, the First National City Bank is on hand to help you in that department.

What Will You Find at the Fair?

The planners who saw to your physical comfort and welfare have done an even better job of catering to your interests. What are the Fair's fabulous 646 acres really like?

Once they held the most appalling sight in a city of appalling sights —the Corona Dumps which Scott Fitzgerald made famous (or infamous) in his "The Great Gatsby." What do they hold today that an expected 70 million tickets will be sold to people who come and come again to gape and take back with them unforgetable memories of an exciting "Brave New World"?

How does one begin to describe a fascinating, fantastic "world of achievement" which has been distilled into a little more than a square mile? If you come to the Fair by way of LaGuardia Airport, your first glimpse of the Fair will be from the air. If you arrive by night, it will be unforgettable. Just below you lies the World's Fair Marina, its glowing satellite centers making an enchanted lagoon of Flushing Bay. To the south shimmers the 646 acres of the Fair, its street lights bright, its myriad fountains and pools sparkling in changing-color spotlights.

Grover Whalen, who —as Robert Moses has put it— was want to borrow his metaphors from Barnum, shown a minature working model of the fountains at the 1939-1940 Fair, reverently remarked that it was the nearest thing to "chaos" that he had ever seen. Were he around to see the fountains of the 1964-1965 Fair, he would have to admit with still more reverence that here was real "chaos." The Fountain of the Planets (in the Pool of Industry) alone has over 1000 jets of water, some reaching as high as 150 feet. Add to this 1300 colored spotlights, gas flames 40 feet high, smoke, pyrotechnic displays and music and the effect produced is a burst of color, water and sound which might well be described as chaotically spectacular —if it weren't that the "chaos" was carefully engineered, controlled and timed to the split second. And this minor "War of the Worlds" occurs nightly for the benefit of the Fair visitors.

If you arrive by land, you will first be struck by the colorful entrance towers, 60 and 80-foot high columns of multi-colored prisms; in the air, the sound of low background music —a music that (integrated with the street lights) will follow you along the principal avenues and promenades of the Fair. The next impressions follow in quick succession: airy, landscaped avenues and promenades; fountains and pools —almost every pavilion boasts of its own— sparkling in the sun; and everywhere, the fantastic fruits of architectural imagination —pavilions, all sizes, all shapes, all colors waiting for you to enter.

At one end of the central promenade, almost at the geographical center of the Fair, stands the Unisphere®, an open globe of the world, its sculptured steel continents affixed to latitudes and longitudes of steel, rising some 12 imposing stories high out of a reflecting pool. Behind it leaps the Fountain of the Continents. Long after the Fair closes its gates, visitors to the "new" Flushing Meadow Park will have this symbol of peace and unity through understanding to remind them of the 12 memorable months New York City played landlord (for the annual rent of an anachronistic dollar) to the achievements, hopes and aspirations of the world's peoples. Around this imposing symbol, within the radius of about half a mile, are clustered the 175 or so pavilions that make up this wonderful world. Fair planners have divided these pavilions into five categorical areas —the International Area, the Federal and State Area, the Industrial Area, the Transportation Area and the Lake Amusement Area.

Since it would take at least a full volume to do justice to all the pavilions at the Fair, only thumbnail sketches of the more outstanding ones follows. Where a pavilion features a restaurant, special entertainment and/or special facilities or exhibits for children, these features are indicated by the following symbols (in parenthesis) next to the name of the exhibitor:

    c - special facilities or exhibits for children

    e - entertainment (either live or in the form of a filmed or animated show)

    r - restaurant—specializing in food of the region.

International Area

AFRICA (Union Africaine et Malgache (cer): History, culture, achievements plus rare art treasures from these ancient lands. Native handicrafts sold. Performances of native dancers. Zoo of African animals for tots and even Mom and Dad. "Tree" restaurant.

BELGIUM (er): An entire Belgium village complete with 124 typical village homes, a church, town hall and shops featuring Belgian craftsmen and handicrafts. Folk dances and Flemish plays given daily at public squares. Rathskellar, ice cream parlor.

CARIBBEAN (er): Exhibits on commercial, industrial and touristic aspects of Caribbean "island paradises," plus display of native handicrafts. Restaurant features Caribbean specialties in food, beverages, entertainment and atmosphere.

CHINA (Republic of): Priceless collection of rare Chinese *objets d'art* covering 40 centuries of Chinese culture. Includes an inscribed tortoise shell showing the beginnings of first written language in Far East. Samples of tea, food.

DENMARK (cr): Emphasis on Danish products and handicrafts plus displays of Danish sculpture and paintings. Children's playground where they may scribble on walls, turn over furniture, etc. (under supervision). Moderate and luxury restaurants.

FRANCE (er): The Latest in French fashions, industrial and consumer goods, French art and culture including a night-club as French as New York City's morals code will allow. Top French entertainers. French restaurant, of course.

GUINEA (er): Circular huts patterned after traditional buildings house native craftsmen producing handicrafts sold in shops. Restaurant features entertainment by Guinea's famous ballet troupe.

HALL OF FREE ENTERPRISE: Exhibits (sponsored by the American Economic Foundation) show how free enterprise operates in a competitive society and how and why it is superior to other economic systems.

HONG KONG (er): Shops and bazaars featuring pearls, "instant clothing," hundreds of other products from one of world's greatest bargain shopping centers. Restaurant-bar and nightclub feature imported Hong Kong entertainment, food.

INDONESIA (er): Native workers busily producing woodcarvings, batik cloths, stone carvings, silver work, etc. Picture tour of archipelago. Restaurant offers spicy Indonesian food to background music of native gamelan and kerontjong orchestras.

INTERNATIONAL PLAZA (r): Burma, Nepal and 14 foreign companies have individual exhibits in a complex of 16 buildings. Handicrafts and other consumer products on display and for sale. Snack-type restaurants.

IRELAND (r): Irish culture, history, economy exhibits. Names and places of origin of all Irish families who migrated to America. Exhibit tracing the evolution of the Irish language. Outdoor restaurant features snacks and "Irish coffee."

ISRAEL (r): Tour through 4000 years of Jewish history starting with a walk through an ancient city and the Holy land and ending in modern Israel. Shopping mall sells arts, crafts, food. Snack bar features kosher and Israeli food.

JAPAN (er): History and culture displays in adaptation of Japanese feudal castle. Modern Japanese products on display and sold. Theater features movies, plays, traditional dancers, and art of tea ceremony, flower arranging and wood blocks. Moderate and deluxe Japanese-style restaurants and snack bar.

KOREA (er): Ancient Korean ceramics, sculptures, paintings, etc. Over 800 Korean products from grand pianos to traditional Korean handicrafts. Films and photos depicting life in Korea. Live Korean folk dancing. Restaurant plus snack bar.

JORDAN (r): Dead Sea Scrolls and stained glass panels of the Stations of the Cross to remind us that Jerusalem and Holy Land are in Jordan. Bazaar displaying and selling typical products and handicrafts, Snack bar.

MALAYSIA (er): Exhibits of native arts and crafts as

well as country's industries, including a scale model of a rubber factory and tin dredge. A theater features a continuous showing of Malaysian films.

MEXICO (er): Aztec sculptures plus other displays on Mexico's cultural heritage and industrial and social progress. Restaurant features hot Mexican food as well as international fare and strolling *mariachi* (Mexican musicians) to entertain.

PAKISTAN (er): Historic displays including rare treasures from recently discovered Indus Valley Civilization; Pakistanis products and handicrafts; models of mausoleum rivaling Taj Mahal and of future capital. Films and fashion shows. Indoor and outdoor restaurant.

POLYNESIA (er): Village on tropical lagoon with native pearl divers, small shops selling native products. Tahitian girls perform traditional dances on outdoor stage. Longhouse restaurant.

SIERRA LEONE (e): Three conical structures echoing the shape of the country's mountain peaks and native rooftops display its history, culture, economy and handicrafts. Native interpretive dancers perform on an elevated stage.

SPAIN (er): Exhibits of Spanish masterpieces including Goya, Velazquez, El Greco, Picasso. Displays of commercial products. Full length films, fashion shows, performances of top Spanish artists such as Segovia given in theater. Three restaurants ranging from inexpensive to deluxe.

SWEDEN (e): Exhibits by some 20 Swedish companies include Sweden's oldest and newest telephone and model of latest jet fighter. "NK" shop sells over 3000 Swedish-made articles at less than $1 up to $100. Smorgasbord restaurant.

THAILAND (r): Pavilion is replica of Thailand's famous Mondot of Saraburi (Shrine of the Dawn) where footprint of Lord Buddha is enshrined. Displays on Thai art, culture, handicrafts plus scenes, information on country. Typical Restaurant.

VATICAN: Michelangelo's incomparably beautiful sculpture, Pietà, in a setting by Broadway's famous Joe Mielziner, plus large color transparencies of the artist's Sistine Chapel. Early Christian sculpture from the catacombs.

Federal and State Area

UNITED STATES (e): Panoramic view of the U.S. via a 15-minute ride produced and run by Cinerama. Museum features American paintings, sculptures, photos. Computer answer questions on likely vacation spots in U.S., etc. American music and performing arts programs given regularly in open mall.

ALASKA: Animated panorama of the state's history, culture, economy, wildlife, beauty and opportunities plus a dramatic presentation of the aurora borealis. Authentic totem poles and record class polar bear also on display.

FLORIDA (cer): Art treasures plus other displays to show what life is like in this "easy-living" citrus state. Porpoise show given ten times daily at outdoor amphitheater by Meadow Lake in Lake Amusement area. Color movies, fashion shows at night.

HAWAII (er): Geological, historical and cultural exhibits, large photographic murals and dioramas, native "village" with craftsmen producing native handicrafts sold at shops. (One features a huge "orchid tree.") Hawaiian music, dances, fashions presented regularly at outdoor theater. Restaurant offers luau and other Hawaiian specialties.

HOLLYWOOD (er): Movie sets from famous films such as "The King and I," "West Side Story," etc. plus a film shooting demonstration in which audience participates. Museum displays mementoes of famous pictures and of career of Cecil B. DeMille.

Admission: Adults—$1.00; children—50c.

ILLINOIS (e): Greatest collection of Lincolniana ever presented at an international event. Featured is a 12-minute Walt Disney-produced "Great Moments with Mr. Lincoln" show in which an electronically animated, life-size Lincoln delivers excerpts from his famous speeches.

MARYLAND (cer): Six-minute film dramatization of the Battle of Fort McHenry which war-prisoner Francis Scott Key witnessed and was inspired to write "The Star Spangled

Banner." Fisherman's Wharf and restaurant offers seafood specialties.

MINNESOTA (r): Unusual pavilion consisting of multiple, hexagonal polyhedrons shaped like the North Star State's symbol features state and industrial displays plus large restaurant offering a menu almost exclusively of Minnesota food.

MISSOURI (r): With "First in Air, First in Space" as theme, exhibit features a replica of Lindbergh's *Spirit of St. Louis* and the Missouri-built Mercury and Gemini space capsules. Open air restaurant offers dishes introduced at St. Louis 1904 World's Fair.

MONTANA (e): Russell and Remington original paintings, gold nugget display and other historical and Indian artifacts from Montana's past on display. Authentic Indian ceremonial dances are performed regularly.

NEW ENGLAND STATES (cer): Complex of state pavilions, New England country store and restaurant centered around a village green show past, present and future of New England States. Fashion shows, Boston Pops concerts, frog-jumping contest, etc. on green.

NEW JERSEY (e): Cluster of pavilions centered around a garden and performing area tell story of N.J.'s 3 centuries of "People, Purpose and Progress." Band concerts, folk dances, choirs, other local talent entertain on "village square."

NEW YORK CITY (e): Huge scale model of New York City with its 840,000 or so buildings and over 100 bridges may be seen via an 8-minute "helicopter" ride (two feet above ground). *Ice-Travaganza* show stars World Champion Don McPherson and large cast.

Admission to ice-skating show: from $1.05 to $2.20.

NEW YORK STATE (er): "Theaterama" features 360° film on New York State. Display of industrial and recreational sites. High point of Fair —230-foot high observatory tower helps you to see as far as New Jersey, Connecticut, Eastern Long Island, Atlantic.

TEXAS (er): Historical, cultural, industrial exhibits plus some six different restaurants scattered throughout site in the

Lake Amusement Area. Texas Music Hall presents tribute to musical comedy in 90 minute "spectacular" show, *To Broadway with Love*.

Admission (all seats reserved): from $2.00 to $4.80.

WEST VIIRGINIA (r): Featured is the "Radio Astronomy Sky" exhibit explaining the work of the National Radio Astronomy Observatory in Green Bank with its radio telescope "on the Universe." "Mountain Lodge" resaturant.

Industrial Area

AMERICAN GAS ASSOCIATION, Inc. (er): Featured: a puppet show in which puppeteer Tom Tichenor (of Broadway hit *Carnival*) manipulates "Tom Therm" in battle against elements; Theater of Food with famous chefs performing; Fun House showing uses of gas from gas worship to kitchen of future; a magic show; "Festival Restaurant '64."

BELL SYSTEM (e): A 12-minute ride, designed and produced by Jo Mielziner, takes you through 50 scenes showing evolution of communications —from primitive drums to today's telestars. Narration over individual loudspeakers.

CHUNKY CANDY ASSOCIATION (c): A "sculptured continuum" of 13 abstract forms which when viewed through peepholes in the forms will line up visually to form whole sculptures —i.e., a giraffe, a horse, etc. Designed for children but adults will be intrigued, too.

COCA COLA: An around-the-world tour stopping at Hong Kong, the Taj Mahal, harbor of Rio de Janiero, tropical forest in Cambodia, New Orleans with sights, sounds, climatic conditions to make you think you are there. Electronic carillon peals the official Fair time.

CONTINENTAL INSURANCE COMPANIES (c): Special 24-foot outdoor screen presents (in color) great moments of the American Revolution accompanied by original folksongs by Ray Charles. Inside, pavilion features large color transparencies and dioramas on Revolution.

DU PONT (e): A musical revue, "The Wonderful World of Chemistry," (including fashion show featuring designs by

Oleg Cassini and Ceil Chapman) presented in two theatres simultaneously, 40 times daily. Music and lyrics by Michael Brown known for his clever nightclub revues.

DYNAMIC MATURITY: Features goals, activities and achievements of older citizens; art gallery of original Kurd Ard human interest paintings; fortnightly drawing on a free, all-expenses paid trip to Europe; free photo of yourself.

ELECTRIC POWER & LIGHT (e): "The Brightest Show on Earth," a musical fantasy features 3-dimensional, animated figures —including a light bulb bearing a resemblance to Benjamin Franklin—who tell and sing the saga of the investor-owned electric utilities.

EQUITABLE LIFE ASSURANCE COMPANY: A 45-foot demographic map of U.S. lights up whenever and in whichever state a birth or death occurs while an electronic counter keeps a running tally of the U.S.'s total population. Two-way concrete stand allows you to watch demograph and shift to watch nightly fireworks at Pool of Industry.

FORMICA CORPORATION: The hilltop World's Fair Formica House, besides demonstrating the practical application of all Formica laminated plastic products, serves as a showcase for the latest consumer products of 15 leading brand name manufacturers.

GENERAL ELECTRIC CORPORATION: Features the first public demonstration of thermonuclear fusion plus several Walt Disney-produced shows including a "Skydome Spectacular" using the pavilion's dome as a screen, a glimpse into the electrical future via kaleidoscopic mirror effects.

HALL OF EDUCATION (cer): Multi-exhibitor pavilion includes a "school of tomorow," a "cafeteria of tomorrow" a "teaching machines demonstrations" section; Dialogues in Depth with leading personalities informally discussing topics of universal interest. Also featured: Infant Care Center and large outdoor playground.

HOUSE OF GOOD TASTE: Three homes —traditional American, contemporary and modern— in addition to being show pieces serve as showcases for the latest home products.

INTERNATIONAL BUSINESS MACHINES (e): A 15-minute show inside an "Information Machine" shows how computers use simple every-day methods to solve complicated problems. Calypso singers to entertain you while you wait. Computer machine to tell you what else exciting happened on your birth date.

S. C. JOHNSON & SON, Inc. (ce): A 12-minute color film shows how people from all over the world are similar despite differing backgrounds; also, a computer to solve housekeeping problems, shoe-shine machines to shine fair-dusty shoes, amusement center for little ones.

NATIONAL CASH REGISTER COMPANY: Entire contents of King James Bible "micro-encapsulated" so that it fits on a small file card, every word readable under a microscope plus other wonders of NCR micro-encapsulation technique. Computer answers host of questions.

PARKER PEN COMPANY: International Pen Friend Program matches you to a person overseas with similar interests, provides postcard with printed name and address, pen and ink, writing desk. You only have to provide the message and postage.

PAVILION OF AMERICAN INTERIORS: (r): First major presentation exclusively of home furnishings for the entire home with products from over 120 manufacturers. Fourteen regional rooms designed by AID. American craftsmen at work in exhibit of Museum of Contemporary Crafts.

Admission: 50c; children under 12 free.

PEPSI COLA COMPANY: A Walt Disney, 9-minute boat ride *(It's a Small World—A Salute to* UNICEF*)* passes through Disneyesque versions of six continents where electronically-animated children in native dress entertain the riders with folksongs and folk dances.

RADIO CORPORATION OF AMERICA: Demonstrations of how color TV shows are produced and broadcast plus a chance to see yourself on color TV and participate in some of the programs. Fair highlights, special events, news, may be seen on 230 color TV sets throughout the Fair.

RHEINGOLD (Liebmann Breweries) (er): "Little Old New York" in 1904 —complete with cobble-stones, gas lamps, village green, park and bandstand— features exhibits, souvenirs, restaurant, tavern, band concerts and live entertainment at bandstand. Park benches make ringside seats for nightly fireworks of Fair.

F & M SCHAEFER BREWING CO. (r): Replica of Inn at Wetzler where Schaeferian ancestors served their beer two centuries ago; "Corridor of Sports" featuring color transparencies of great sports moments; Schaefer "Restaurant of Tomorrow" and Beer Garden.

THE SCOTT PAPER COMPANY (c): A 15 minute tour through the "Scott Enchanted Forest" tells you the fascinating story of paper from the tree to the finished product. Also featured: "the most luxurious restroom facilities" and a diaper-changing room for harassed mothers with moist toddlers.

SEVEN UP (er): The 7-Up International Sandwich Gardens offers a tray of four sandwiches from four countries plus 7-Up for a flat $1.50. Continuous entertainment by international musical, dancing and comedy acts while you munch sandwiches, sip 7-Up.

THE TRAVELERS INSURANCE COMPANIES: "Triumph of Man" exhibit features thirteen 20-foot wide dioramas —combined with narration, sound effects, animation —showing how man has triumphed over threats to his existence. Journey through 2 million years takes 18 minutes.

UNITED STATES RUBBER CO: An 80-foot high ferris wheel disguised as a U. S. Royal Giant Tire gives you one of the best views of the Fair and Fairgrounds. Displays of U. S. Rubber tire line at base.

WESTINGHOUSE ELECTRIC CORPORATION: Time Capsule II, a twin of Time Capsule I buried 25 years ago at the 1939-1940 New York World's Fair, and its future contents are displayed. Capsule hangs suspended above new monument marking burial site of first twin.

Transporation Area

AUTO THRILL SHOW (e): For thrills go watch 30 "Hell Drivers" near kill themselves at the new stadium specially designed for auto thrill driving. Features fender to fender criss-crossing, reverse spins, broad jumps, "dive bomber crash"—all in cars.

Admission: General—$1.00; Reserved—$1.50.

CHRYSLER CORPORATION (e): Huge walk-through engine houses exhibits on Chrysler engineering; a car shaped building, on Chrysler styling, etc. Theater features continuous musical presentation of Chrysler doings in automotive world and aerospace field.

FORD MOTOR COMPANY (e): A 12-minute, Walt Disney-produced fantasy ride where you'll see prehistoric monsters battling, cavemen lighting fires and talking caveman talk and so on to the city of tomorrow—all life size, 3-dimensional, electronically animated.

GENERAL MOTORS (e): Futurama II ride features GM Staff's educated (and thoroughly realistic) guess as to what's ahead for transportation, not in space but right here on earth. Atop the pavilion sits a 24-foot high time and temperature indicator for the clock- and climate-watchers.

HALL OF SCIENCE (c): A fascinating collection of exhibits on nuclear physics, electronics, the physics of light, etc., including a simulated rendezvous in "outer space" between full scale models of a re-supply rocket and a large space station.

PORT OF NEW YORK AUTHORITY (e): The Fair's heliport. Also features a 13-minute "wrap-around" 360° motion picture of the New York-New Jersey port in action. "Top of the Fair" Restaurant and "Drinks around the World" cocktail lounge provide a panoramic view of Fair.

SINCLAIR REFINING COMPANY: Nine, too-life-like-for-comfort dinosaurs set in a natural habitat of 160 million years ago when they ruled the world. Three are partly animated including the formidable 70-foot long, 20-ton brontosaurus, Sinclair's corporate symbol.

SFK INDUSTRIES, Inc. (e): An 8-minute electronically animated, audio-visual presentation showing how man has progressed with the help of roller and ball bearings. A "wall of motion" displays cutaway forms of products using rolling bearings.

SOCONY MOBILE OIL: A "Driver Game" shows how well you drive via a simulated driver's seat with a workable steering wheel, brakes and accelerator which you operate while shown a motion picture of driving situations occurring on the Mobile Economy Run.

TRANSPORTATION AND TRAVEL: Multi-exhibitor pavilion bursting with travel ideas including a space-flight trip to the moon where you are taken on a sightseeing tour around the rim of a crater, plus a Hall of Fame honoring 20th century pioneers of transportation.

UNDERGROUND WORLD HOME: Complete, modern three-bedroom with patio, terrace, garden area, pure air, air conditioning, freedom from noise and climatic hazards and the ultimate in privacy —enclosed in a concrete shell five feet below ground.

The Lake Amusement Area

The Lake Amusement Area, the Fair's playground, offers something for everyone from the toddling age to the tottering stage. Besides the pavilions of Florida, Hawaii and Texas previously described, you'll find some twelve other rides and shows —all charging admission. (Prices in the Lake Amusement Area range from 50c to $4.80.)

▪ For the tots, the rides and games at **Kiddyland** will send them into ecstatic spasms.

▪ The oldsters will enjoy a restful, 20-minute cruise on Meadow Lake. They may have their pick of a gondola ride in Venice, a cruise on the Mississippi in the "Robert E. Lee" or in a glass-bottom boat through the Florida Keys.

▪ for the young (and strong) of heart, the **Flume Ride**

will give them the thrills of "shooting the rapids" in a floating hollow log . . .

■ . . . or they may want to try the **Jaycopter Ride** giving them the sensation of being in a helicopter going through such complicated maneuvers as flares, hovers, side and reverse flight, spins, drops and climbs.

■ Camera fans will especially appreciate the **Aerial Ride** in a gondola carrying them up to a height of 100 feet. Practically everyone will appreciate the Belgian waffles served in the restaurant at the base of the gondola tower.

■ For those who want a close but bird's eye view of the Lake Amusement Area and environs, the **Monorail Ride** ("tomorrow's mass transportation system")—making a complete loop of the Fair at a height of 40 feet—is for them.

■ The entire family —especially the youngsters— should enjoy John Ringling North's one ring **Continental Circus** with its share of spine tingling aerialist and tightrope walker acts. Everyone will enjoy the daily Circus Parade.

■ Anyone appreciating color and action will find the **Dancing Waters** 20-minute show breathtaking. 4000 jets of water, multi-colored lights and music, create effects ranging from "fireworks" display to a classical ballet scene.

■ For the student there's the completely authentic replica of that 15th century spaceship, Columbus' flagship the **Santa Maria,** docked at a 15th century wharf. In the hold, are dioramas depicting highlights in the life of Columbus.

■ For the curious, the Walter's International Wax **Museum** has over 30 life-size tableaux in scenes ranging from the historical to the contemporary—from Cleopatra, in fact, to President Lyndon B. Johnson.

■ Americans should enjoy the **American Indian Village** featuring authentic American Indian ceremonial dances, a "Trading Post," Indian art and culture, Indian life on a reservation with Indian craftsmen at work.

■ If you're looking for a "Hollywood Spectacular," try the **Wonderworld** show featuring a cast of 250 performing on land, sea and air, the largest revolving stage in America, a giant waterfall and the launching of a Lady Astronaut.

- For adult entertainment in the grand but somewhat miniaturized manner, there's **Les Poupees de Paris** billed as that "naughty French puppet revue" with a cast of 250 puppets and a wardrobe that includes a $15,000 chinchilla coat.

In addition to the exhibits already described, there are a group of pavilions which don't rightly belong in any of the five areas though they are found among them (mostly in the international Area). These pavilion belong to various religious and civic groups, including the following:

- The **Boy Scouts of America** exhibit (in the Industrial Area) —"The Wonderful World of Scouting"— featuring exhibits on Scouting's purpose and program including demonstrations of scouting skills.

- The **Church of Jesus Christ of the Latter Day Saints** pavilion duplicating the façade of Salt Lake City's famous Mormon Temple, features immense mural on Mormon history and a marble replica of "The Christus" by Bertel Rebechi.

- The **Garden of Meditation** where you'll find —just as its name implies— a garden oasis of peace and quiet and granite boulders inscribed with biblical references to help you mediate.

- The **Masonic Brotherhood Foundation** depicting the part the Masonic order has played in the history of New York and of the U. S. including a 13-foot model of George Washington in full mason regalia.

- The **Protestant and Orthodox Center** with a forecourt honoring protestant pioneers, exhibits by 16 major protestant and orthodox religions, a wide-screen evangelistic film, an outdoor childrens play center.

- The **Russian Orthodox-Greek Catholic Church** chapel in which is enshrined the five-century old Miraculous Ikon of Our Lady of Kazan encrusted with more than 1000 jewels including diamonds, rubies, pearls and sapphires.

Appendix

Hotels

Adams Hotel
2 E. 86th St. RH 4-1800; 12.00-16.00; 18.00-22.00

Alamac Hotel
71st St. & Broadway. EN 2-5000; 6.00-8.50; 9.00-10.00

Albert Hotel
23 E. 10th St. OR 7-0100; 6.00-10.00; 7.00-12.00

Algonquin Hotel
59 W. 44th St. MU 7-4400; 10.50-17.00; 14.50-20.50

Alrae Hotel
37 E. 64th St. RH 4-0200; 16.00-20.00; 20.00-26.00

America Hotel
145 W. 47th St. CO 5-6300; 6.00-7.00; 10.00-13.00

Americana of New York
52nd St. & 7th Ave. LT 1-1000; 14.00-23.00; 16.00-32.00

Arlington Hotel
18 W. 25th St. WA 9-8960; 5.00-8.00; 6.00-12.00

Astor Hotel
44th St. & Broadway. JU 6-3000; 10.00-18.00; 15.00-23.00

Barbizon-Plaza Hotel
106 Central Park S. CI 7-7000; 10.50-16.50; 16.50-25.00

Beekman Hotel
575 Park Ave. TE 8-4900; 18.00-21.00; 23.00-26.00

Beekman Tower Hotel
3 Mitchell Pl. EL 5-7300; 9.00-14.00; 14.00-20.00

Belmont Plaza Hotel
49th St. at Lexington Ave. PL 5-1200; 11.00-16.00; 14.00-22.00

Biltmore Hotel
43rd St. at Madison Ave. MU 7-7000; 14.95-21.95; 18.95-26.95

Blackstone Hotel
50 E. 58th St. EL 5-4200; 10.00-12.00; 12.00-14.00

Bolivar Hotel
230 Central Park W. SU 7-6000; 8.00-10.00; 10.00-14.00

Buckingham Hotel
101 W. 57th St. CI 6-1500; 10.50-12.50; 12.50-16.50

Cameron Hotel
41 W. 86th St. SC 4-6900; 6.00-10.00; 10.00-18.00

Carlyle Hotel
35 E. 76th St. RH 4-1600; 20.00-28.00; 24.00-35.00

Carriage House Hotel
200 E. 38th St. MO 1-2100; 15.00-18.00; 17.00-20.00

Carteret Hotel
208 W. 23rd St. WA 9-7060; 5.00-8.00; 7.00-10.00

Claridge Hotel
44th St. & Broadway. JU 2-5050; 8.00-10.00; 10.00-14.00

Coliseum House
228 W. 71st St. TR 3-1000; 5.00-9.00; 8.00; 14.00

Collingwood Hotel
45 W. 35th St. WI 7-2500; 7.00-12.00; 10.00-16.00

Commodore Hotel
42nd St. at Park & Lexington Aves. MU 6-600
11.00-20.00; 16.00-23.00

Croydon Hotel
12 E. 86th St. BU 8-4000; 10.00-12.00; 14.00-16.00

Delmonico Hotel
502 Park Ave. EL 5-2500; 17.00-24.00; 22.00-28.00

Dorset Hotel
30 W. 54th St. CI 7-7300; 16.00-21.00; 22.00-26.00

Drake Hotel
440 Park Ave. PL 5-0600; 18.00-23.00; 26.00-30.00

Empire Hotel
63rd St. & Broadway. CO 5-7400; 7.00-10.00; 10.00-16.00

Esplanade Hotel
305 West End Ave. TR 4-5000; 9.00-12.00; 10.00-16.00

Essex House
160 Central Park S. CI 7-0300; 16.00-31.00; 20.00-31.00

Excelsior Hotel
45 W. 81st St. EN 2-9200; 11.00; 14.00

Executive Hotel
237 Madison Ave. MU 6-0300; 12.50-15.50; 15.50-21.00

Fifth Avenue Hotel
24 5th Ave. GR 3-6400; 12.00-16.00; 17.00-20.00

George Washington Hotel
23rd St. & Lexington Ave. GR 5-1920; 7.50-11.00; 13.00-16.50

Gladstone Hotel
 114 E. 52nd St. PL 3-4300; 13.00-19.00; 17.00-23.00
Gorham Hotel
 136 W. 55th St. CI 5-1800; 12.00-15.00; 14.00-18.00
Gotham Hotel
 700 5th Ave. CI 7-2200; 14.00-20.00; 19.00-30.00
Governor Clinton Hotel
 371 7th Ave. PE 6-3400; 8.00-15.50; 10.00-21.00
Gramercy Park Hotel   *would be fun sort of near Village*
 Lexington Ave. & 21st St. GR 5-4320; 11.50-15.00; 14.50-19.00
Great Northern Hotel
 118 W. 57th St. CI 7-1900; 8.00-12.00; 11.00-15.00
Greystone Hotel
 212 W. 91st St. SC 4-1800; 6.00-7.00; 9.00-11.00
Grosvenor Hotel
 35 5th Ave. GR 3-6000; 9.50-12.00; 13.50-16.00
Hampshire House
 150 Central Park S. CI 6-7700; 18.00-28.00; 22.00-28.00
Henry Hudson Hotel
 353 W. 57th St. CO 5-6100; 7.00-12.00; 10.00-16.00
Holland Hotel
 351 W. 42nd St. CI 6-0700; 6.00; 8.00-9.00
Kenmore Hotel   *No*
 145 E. 23rd St. GR 5-3840; 5.50-6.50; 8.00-12.00
Lancaster Hotel
 22 E. 38th St. (Madison Ave.) MU 5-3700; 8.50-18.00; 12.00-23.00
Le Marquis Hotel
 12 E. 31st St. MU 4-7480; 5.00-7.00; 7.00-9.00
Lexington Hotel
 Lexington Ave. & E. 48th St. PL 5-4400; 11.00-16.25; 15.25-21.25
Lincoln Square Hotel
 166 W. 75th St. TR 3-3000; 5.00-8.00; 7.00-12.00
Lombardy Hotel
 111 E. 56th St. PL 3-8600; 25.00-30.00; 30.00-35.00
Madison Square Hotel
 35 Madison Ave. LE 2-6880; 6.00; 7.00-8.00
Manger Vanderbilt Hotel
 Park Ave., at 34th St. MU 3-4000; 9.00-23.00; 14.00-23.00
Manhattan Towers Hotel
 Broadway & 76th St. SU 7-1900; 6.00-10.00; 10.00-15.00

Mansfield Hotel
    12 W. 44th St. MU 2-5140; 7.00-9.00; 8.00-12.00
Murray Hill Hotel
    42 W. 35th St. WI 7-0200; 8.00-12.00; 11.00-15.00
Nassau Hotel
    56 E. 59th St. EL 5-3250; 5.00-6.00; 8.00-10.00
National Hotel
    592 7th Ave. (42nd St.) WI 7-3800; 6.00-7.00; 9.00; 10.00
Navarro Hotel
    112 Central Park S. CI 7-7900; 16.50-22.00; 19.50-26.00
New Weston Hotel
    50th St. & Madison Ave. PL 3-4800; 13.00-19.00; 19.00-25.00
New York Hilton at Rockefeller Center *Superb !!!*
    Ave. of the Americas, 53rd & 54th Sts. JU 6-7000
       14.00-24.00; 18.00-32.00
New Yorker Hotel *no?*
    34th St. & 8th Ave. LO 3-1000; 9.00-12.00; 12.00-17.00
Olcott Hotel
    27 W. 72nd St. TR 7-4200; 8.00-12.00; 10.00-16.00
One Fifth Avenue Hotel
    1 5th Ave. SP 7-7000; 13.00-17.00; 16.00-20.00
Paramount Hotel
    235 W. 46th St. CI 6-5500; 8.00-12.00; 12.00-18.00
Paris Hotel
    752 West End Ave. RI 9-3500; 5.00-9.00; 7.50-14.50
Park Crescent Hotel
    150 Riverside Dr. TR 3-6200; 9.00-15.00; 12.00-20.00
Park Lane Hotel
    299 Park Ave. PL 5-4100; 19.50-23.00; 25.50-29.00
Park Plaza Hotel
    50 W. 77th St. SU 7-5900; 4.50-6.00; 7.00-10.00
Penn Terminal Hotel
    215 W. 34th St. WI 7-5050; 7.00-8.00; 9.00-11.00
Pickwick Arms Hotel
    230 E. 51st St. EL 5-0300; 6.25-6.75; 9.50-10.50
Pierre Hotel
    1 E. 61st St. TE 8-8000; 23.00-28.00; 28.00-34.00
Plaza Hotel
    5th Ave. at 59th St. PL 9-3000; 15.00-25.00; 20.00-34.00

Regency Hotel
Park Ave. at 61st St. PL 9-4100; 22.00-32.00; 26.00-36.00
28 E. 31st St. (Madison Ave.) MU 9-0600; 8.50-14.50; 10.50-14.50

Roosevelt Hotel
45th St. at Madison Ave. MU 6-9200; 12.95-19.95; 16.95-24.95

Rosoff's Hotel
147 W. 43rd St. JU 2-3200; 4.00-7.00; 7.00-12.00

Ruxton Hotel
50 W. 72nd St. SU 7-0500; 8.00-10.00; 10.00-12.00

St. Moritz Hotel
50 Central Park S. PL 5-5800; 13.00-20.00; 16.00-25.00

St. Regis Hotel
2 E. 55th St. PL 3-4500; 15.00-27.00; 24.00-32.00

Salisbury Hotel *nol*
123 W. 57th St. CI 6-1300; 12.00-15.00; 17.00-20.00

San Carlos Hotel
150 E. 50th St. PL 5-1800; 13.00-18.00; 16.00-23.00

Savoy Hilton Hotel *good*
5th Ave. & 58th St. EL 5-2600; 12.00-25.00; 17.00-30.00

Seton Hotel
144 E. 40th St. MU 5-2445; 12.00-14.00; 13.00-15.00

Seville Hotel
22 E. 29th St. LE 2-2960; 6.00-10.00; 8.50-12.00

Shelburne Hotel
303 Lexington Ave. MU 9-5200; 10.85-13.85; 13.85-16.85

Shelton Towers Hotel
Lexington Ave. 48th-49th Sts. PL 5-4000; 9.85-14.85; 12.85-17.85

Sheraton Atlantic Hotel
34th St. & Broadway. PE 6-5700; 10.75-16.00; 14.75-20.00

Stanford Hotel
155 W. 22nd St. OR 5-7333; 12.00-15.00; 12.00-15.00

Stanhope Hotel
995 5th Ave. BU 8-5800; 16.00-24.00; 20.00-28.00

Statler-Hilton Hotel *no*
401 7th Ave. PE 6-5000; 10.00-19.00; 14.00-25.00

Summit Hotel
E. 51st St. & Lexington Ave. PL 2-7000; 14.00-28.00; 16.00-32.00

Surrey Hotel
20 E. 76th St. RH 4-1690; 19.00-22.00; 23.00-26.00

Taft Hotel
  7th Ave. at 50th St. CI 7-4000; 8.50-14.25; 12.50-19.25
Theresa Hotel
  2090 7th Ave. (125th St.) UN 6-3300; 9.65-11.75; 9.65-13.77
Tudor Hotel
  304 E. 42nd St. YU 6-8800; 7.00-11.00; 10.00-17.00
Tuscany Hotel
  39th St. E. of Park Ave. MU 6-1600; 19.80-25.80; 25.80-31.80
Victoria Hotel
  51st St. & 7th Ave. CI 7-7800; 8.50-12.00; 12.00-18.00
Van Rensselaer Hotel
  15 E. 11th St. AL 5-6660; 6.00-7.00; 8.00-16.00
Waldorf-Astoria Hotel
  301 Park Ave. EL 5-3000; 10.00-27.00; 16.00-32.00
Westover Hotel
  253 W. 72nd St. EN 2-9600; 8.00-10.00; 10.00-12.00
Windermere Hotel
  666 West End Ave. SC 4-8200; 8.00-9.50; 8.00-12.50

Motels

City Squire Motor Inn
  51st St. & Broadway. LT 1-3300; 14.00-22.00; 16.00-26.00
Holiday Inn of New York City
  57th St.-9th & 10th Aves. LT 1-8100; 13.00-22.00; 17.00-26.00
Howard Johnson's Motor Lodge
  51st St. & 8th Ave. LT 1-4100; 12.00-20.00; 14.00-26.00
Lincoln Square Motor Inn
  155 W. 66th St. SU 7-6800; 12.00-22.00; 14.00-24.00
Loew's Midtown Motor Inn
  48th St. & 8th Ave. LT 1-7000; 13.00-21.00; 15.00-25.00
Motel City
  510 W. 42nd St. OX 5-7171; 14.00-16.00; 16.00-22.00
Riviera Congress Motor Inn
  550 10th Ave. OX 5-3100; 12.00-20.00; 16.00-24.00
Sheraton Motor Inn
  12th Ave. at 42nd St. OX 5-6500; 11.50-13.75; 13.75-21.00
Skyline Motor Inn
  725 10th Ave. JU 6-3400; 14.00-20.00; 14.00-20.00
Times Square Motor Hotel
  255 W. 43rd St. LA 4-6900; 8.00-10.50; 11.00-16.50

Restaurants

A

Al Schacht 102 East 52nd St., PL 9-8570
American. Steaks, chops, seafood. Sports celebrities spot. A la carte lunch from $2.25; dinner from $3.25. Closed for lunch Sat. & Sun.

Albert French 42 East 11th St., OR 3-3890
American. All the steak you can eat for $2.85. Lunch and dinner from $2.85. Free tour of Greenwich Village.

B

Balkan Armenian 129 East 27th St., MU 9-7925
Armenian only. Shish Kebab, tourlu guevech, lamp shank. A la carte lunch from $1.45; dinner from $1.70; seven course dinner from $3.50. Closed Sun. Closes 9 p.m.

Brasserie 100 East 53rd St., PL 1-4840
French-Alsatian. Quiche Lorraine, escargots Bourguignon, beekenohfe. Lunch from $1.95; dinner from $4.50. Service bar only. Open 24 hours a day all year round. French background music and Picasso plates for decor. Under Restaurants Associates management.

Brauhaus 249 East 86th St., LE 4-9840
German-continental. Sauerbraten, pigs knuckle, wiener schnitzel, steak. Lunch from $1.75; dinner from $2.50; a la carte lunch & dinner from $1.25. Dancing and entertainment.

C

Café Arnold 240 Central Park So., CI 6-7050
French. Squab chicken Veronique, filet mignon with Sauce Béarnaise. A la carte lunch from $1.50; dinner from $4.50. Closed Sundays. Background music.

Café Chambord-à la Cote Basque 5 East 55th St., EL 5-7180
French (one of the best). Le homard des gourmets flambé a l'absinthe, bouillabaise, soufflé grand marnier. All a la carte. Lunch from $3; dinner from $4.50. Opens Sun. after 5 p.m.

Café Louis XIV 15 East 49th St., CI 6-5800
French. A la carte lunch from $2.25; dinner from $3.50. Complete table d'hote $7.50. Strolling violinist and piano music at dinner.

Captain's Table 410 Sixth Ave., AL 4-6825
Seafood. Red Snapper en papilotte. Lunch from $1.40; dinner a la carte from $1.70.

Cavanagh's   256 West 23rd St., AL 5-1100
American. Steaks, cornish hen, baked sole. Lunch from $3.25; dinner from $4.25. A la carte also available. Complete dinner includes shrimp cocktail, garlic bread, dessert à la mode at no extra charge. One of New York's oldest, respected restaurants.

Chardas   307 East 79th St., RH 4-9382
Hungarian. Paprika chicken, Hungarian goulash. Dinner from $5.75, à la carte from $4.50. Dancing to gypsy orchestra. Entertainment tax after 9:30 p.m. Closed Mon.

Chinese Rathskeller   45 Mott St., WO 2-8943
Chinese. Winter melon soup, chow steak kow, lobster Cantonese. Lunch from $1.10; dinner from $1.85 Also à la carte.

The Coach House   110 Waverly Place, SP 7-0303
American — Southern Style. Prime ribs of beef, lobster, cornish hen, black bean soup. Lunch from $2.00; dinner from $4.75. A la carte lunch from $1.50; dinner from $3.75. No bar.

The Cottage   132 West 32nd St., LO 5-4838
American-Italian. Home style cooking in homey colonial atmosphere. Popular shoppers spot. Lunch from 99c; dinner from $1.75. A la carte lunch from 85c; dinner from $1.50. No bar. Open for breakfast. Closed Sun.

D

Danny's Hide-A-Way   151 East 45th St., YU 6-5350
Italian-American. Filet mignon, lobster, duck, veal parmigiana. A la carte lunch from $2.10; dinner from $4.00. Closed Sun.

Dardanelles Armenian   86 University Place, CH 2-8990
Armenian. Shish kebab, stuffed mussels and grape leaves. Lunch from $1.95; dinner from $3.25. A la carte lunch from $1.35; dinner from $1.75.

Davy Jones   103 West 49th St., JU 6-2936
Seafood. King crabs, stone crabs, lobster. Lunch from $1.65. A la carte dinner from $2.75.

E

Eberlin's   45 New St., DI 4-6237
American. One of New York's oldest restaurants catering to the financial district crowd. Lunch from $1.25; dinner from $1.50; a la carte from $1.50. Closed Sat. & Sun.

Exchange Restaurant   541 Madison Ave., PL 3-8624
American. Fish cakes, broiled lobster, home-made pies and layer cakes. Owned by New York Exchange for Women's Work and full of hand-made samples. A la carte lunch from $1.35; dinner from $2.50. Closed Sun. Closed Sat. for dinner.

F

Felix's   154 West 13th St., CH 3-9767
Italian. Veal cutlet à la parmigiana, lobster à la fra diablo.
Lunch from $1.50; dinner from $2.95. Closed Sun.

Forno's   236 West 52nd St., CI 7-9420
Spanish-Latin American. Paella a la Valenciana, pampano papil-
lot, suckling pig. A la carte from $1.75 to $3.75. Closed Mon.

The Forum of the Twelve Caesars   57 West 48th St., PL 7-3450
International cuisine with an ancient Roman touch. "Pliny's
Baked Chicken in Clay," etc. Very plush decor. Plushier prices.

Four Seasons   99 East 52nd St., PL 1-4300
International cuisine and decor change with the seasons. New
York's most luxurious. A la carte lunch from $3.25; dinner from
$4.50; $1.00 cover. Closed Sun.

Fraunces Tavern   54 Pearl St., BO 9-0144
American. New York's oldest restaurant and historical landmark where George Washington bade farewell to his officers in
1783. Lunch from $1.85; dinner from $2.00. Closed Sun.

G

Golden Horn   122 West 49th St., CI 6-0870
Armenian-Turkish-American. Shish kebab, chicken and oriental
wild rice, ajem pilaff. *Holiday* named this one among America's
103 great restaurants. Lunch from $1.75; dinner from $3.50. A la
carte lunch from $1.50; dinner from $2.50.

Granson's   525 Lexington Ave., PL 5-9688
American-International. Seafood and oyster bars, prime ribs of
beef, steaks. Luncheon specials include daily international lunch.
Lunch from $1.35; dinner from $2.75. A la carte lunch from $1.25;
dinner from $2.15.

Gripsholm   324 East 57th St., PL 9-6260
Swedish. Smorgasbord, Swedish pancakes. Lunch from $2.50, din-
ner from $3.75. Smörgasbord, dessert & coffee for lunch $2.75; for
dinner $4.25.

Grotto Azzurra   387 Broome St., CA 6-9283
Neopolitan. Lobster fra diavolo, veal rollatini alla marsala,
stripped bass. A la carte lunch, dinner from $1.75. Closed Mon.

H

Hapsburg House   313 East 55th St., PL 3-5169
Viennese-Continental. Esterhazy tokany, chicken cutlet Mercedes,
tournedos Alex. Founded by Ludwig Bemelmans and decorated
with his lighthearted sketches. Zither music in the evenings. A
garden dining room in the summer. Lunch from $1.50; dinner
from $4.75. A la carte lunch from $1.50. Closed Sun.

Harvey's Seafood House　　　　509 Third Avenue, MU 3-7587

Seafood-steaks-chops. Lobster, Alaskan king crab, pompano, brook trout, oyster pot pie, baked fish loaf, bouillabaisse. A la carte lunch from $1.45; dinner from $1.95.

Hearthstone　　　　　　　　102 East 22nd St., GR 5-1889

American. Fried chicken, lobster pie, old fashioned lamb stew and roast beef, home made pies and hot bread. Lunch from $1.15; dinner from $1.75. Closed Sun. Closed July 3-22 and Sat. in July & August.

Holland House Taverne　　　10 Rockefeller Plaza, CI 6-5800

Dutch-Javanese. Javanese rice curry. A la carte lunch from $1.95; dinner from $3.95. Closed Sun.

House of Chan　　　　　52nd St. & Seventh Ave., PL 7-4470

Chinese. Lobster wor, mandarin duck, asparagus steak kew, spareribs. Lunch from $1.30. A la carte dinner from $2.25.

J

Jai Alai　　　　　　　　　82 Bank St., CH 3-9448

Spanish. Paella a la Valenciana, caldo gallego, clams Jai Alai, mariscala a la bilbaina. Lunch from $1.55; dinner from $2.50; paella a la Valenciana $3.50. A la carte lunch and dinner from $2.00. Closed Sun.

Janssen's　　　　　　　430 Lexington Ave., LE 2-5661

German-Continental. Rahmschnitzel, sauerbraten, alpenragout, all game in season. Nuremberg panels, antique ship models, paintings and murals add charming atmosphere. Lunch from $2.25; dinner from $4.25. A la carte lunch from $2.10; dinner from $2.25. Nightly violin & accordian music. Closed Sun.

Joe King's German-American Rathskeller

190 Third Ave., GR 5-7623

German-American. Deutscher sauerbraten. Piano music for nightly community singing. Favorite with the college crowd. A la carte from $2.00. Open for dinner only from 4:30 p.m. to 4 a.m.

Joy Young　　　　　　　　65 Mott St., BE 3-9404

Chinese. Hop tow gai ding. Lunch from 75c; dinner from $1.30. A la carte lunch from 65c, dinner from $1.30. Family dinner, $2.25.

K

Kabuki　　　　　　　　135 Broadway, WO 2-4677

Japanese. Sukiyaki, tempura, mizutaki, teishoku (complete Japanese dinner). Lunch from $2.25, dinner from $4.50. A la carte lunch from $1.75; dinner from $2.25. Background music.

Karachi　　　　　　　　144 West 46th St., CI 5-9643

Indian-Pakistani. Shish kebab, curried dishes, Indian bread. Unpretensious but notable. Lunch from 95c; dinner from $2.00. A la carte lunch & dinner from $1.15. Closed Sun. during summer.

Keen's English Chop House 72 West 36th St., WI 7-3636
English-American. English mutton chops, roast beef, steak, Yorkshire pudding. A New York landmark, established since 1876. Churchwarden Pipe Club collection on display. Lunch from $2.10; dinner from $4.25. A la carte also. Closed Sun.

L

La Fonda del Sol 123 West 50th St., PL 7-8800
Latin American. Bocaditos de la Fonda del Sol, churrasco a la criolla, anticuchos mixtos, farofa, asado de tira barbacoa, matambre. The decor —colorful Indian and folk art of Latin America— alone is worth a visit. Four-course lunch, $4.50; seven course dinner, $7.00. A la carte lunch & dinner from $1.95. Brunch, $4.00. Entertainment Sun.

Larre's 50 West 56th St., CI 7-8980
French-continental. Roast duckling bigarade, escargots de Bourgogne, frogs legs provençale, filet mignon with mushroom sauce. Lunch from $1.50; dinner from $3.00. Closed Sun.

Le Boeuf à la Mode 539 East 81st St., RH 4-9232
French. Boeuf à la mode, of course. Lunch from $2.25. A la carte dinner from $3.25. Closed Sun.

Le Marmiton 41 East 49th St., MU 8-1232
French. Steak au poivre, cote de veau aux cepes, lobster St. Honore. Lunch from $3.75; dinner from $4.90. Closed Sun. Closed Sat. as well from June 1st to Labor Day. Dinner music.

Le Pavillon 111 East 57th St., PL 3-8388
French. Considered one of the country's finest if not the finest French restaurant and one of the world's great. Everything served is a "specialty." Lunch from $7.50. A la carte lunch from $3.75; dinner from $4.50. Reservations a must. Closed Sun.

Les Pyrenées 234 West 48th St., CI 6-0044
French. Escalop of veal Basquaise, boeuf braise Beaunoise, roast duck with black cherries. Lunch from $2.00, dinner from $4.25.

Liborio 150 West 47th St., JU 2-6188, JU 6-9009
Latin American. Feijoada Brasileira, tutú de feijao, enchiladas mexicanas, milaneza Argentina, paella valenciana, ropa vieja. Lunch from $1.75. A la carte lunch from $2.00; dinner from $5.00. Minimum charge after 8 p.m. Nightly entertainment featuring top Latin American & Spanish talent, two orchestras, dancing.

The Lichee Tree 65 East 8th St., GR 5-0555
Chinese. Sizzling go ba, ho go-Chinese fire pot. Lunch from $1.50; dinner from $2.75. A la carte lunch & dinner from $1.50.

Limelight 91 Seventh Ave. So., OR 5-2212
International. Shish kebab, Limelight pizza. Dinner from $1.80.

Sunday brunch 11 a.m. to 4 p.m., from $1.00 to $1.50. Sunday buffet 5 to 10 p.m., $2.25 for all you can eat. Not open for lunch.

Lindy's   1655 Broadway, CO 5-0288

American. After theater spot for theater people. Cheese cake a must. Also chicken-in-the pot, blintzes. Lunch from $1.65. A la carte dinner from $1.85.

Luau 400   400 East 57th St., EL 5-6555

Hawaiian-Polynesian. Roast kalua suckling pig, chicken Tahiti, lobster Sayonara, lau-lau, chicken moki, shrimp Balinese. Music by Hal Aloma trio. Luau, $6.75. Dinner a la carte from $2.00. Open for cocktails and dinner only.

Lüchow's   110 East 14th St., GR 7-4860

German-Viennese. Sauerbraten, wiener schnitzel, game in season. A New York landmark —one of New York's oldest and most celebrated restaurants. Gay atmosphere. Music from 7 to 10 p.m. Lunch from $1.75; dinner from $3.75. A la carte lunch and dinner from $2.35. Closed Mon.

M

Mamma Leone's   239 West 48th St., JU 5-5151

Italian. Antipasto, fettucine, home made manicotti, filetto di bue, cassata a la Siciliana, zabaione. Music & entertainment. Dinner from $5.00. A la carte supper (11:30 p.m. to closing) from $1.50. Open for dinner only.

Mandarin House, Inc.   133 West 13th St., WA 9-0551

Chinese. Chicken with walnuts, moo sue juo, west lake duck. Lunch from $1.35; dinner from $2.85. A la carte lunch & dinner from $2.25. Closed Thanksgiving.

Mayan   16 West 51st St., CI 6-5800

International-American. A different international dish every day. Ancient Mayan decor. Lunch from $1.95; dinner from $3.25. A la carte also available. Closed Sun.

McSorley's Old Ale House   15 East 7th St., GR 7-9363

American. Corned beef & cabage, roast pork, roast beef. Over a century old. A New York City landmark and only tavern left *for men only*. Lunch & dinner from $1.00.

Miller's Restaurants   144 Fulton St., WO 2-8077
    233 Broadway, CO 7-3156

American-Continental. Beef à la mode, steaks and chops. Three generations of Millers have served New Yorkers. A la carte lunch from $1.95. Dinner from $2.00. Closed Sat., Sun. & legal holidays.

Miyako's   20 West 56th St., CO 5-3177

Japanese. Beef sukiyaki cooked at your table, tempura, bean soup. Lunch from $2.50; dinner from $3.00. Closed Mon. Open Sun. at 5 p.m.

Mona Lisa   69-71 MacDougal St., GR 3-9804
Italian. Boneless chicken a la parmigiana, home made manicotti
and ravioli, gnocchi. Dinner from $2.90. A la carte lunch from
$1.00; dinner from $1.10. Closed Sun.

Moskowitz & Lupowitz   40 Second St., GR 7-9500
Roumanian-Jewish. Charcoal broiled steak, roast goose with
browned kasha, stuffed derma, goose pastrami, knishes, mushk
steak. Gay atmosphere, gypsy string trio. Lunch from $1.50; dinner
from $3.50. A la carte lunch & dinner from $2.50.

O

O Henry's Steak House   345 Sixth Ave., CH 2-2000
American. Charcoal broiled steaks, chops, spare ribs, seafood.
Little old New York atmosphere with gas lamps, waiters in straw
hats & butcher aprons and strawdust on the floor. Lunch from
$1.55; dinner from $2.95.

Old Brew House   207 East 54th St., EL 5-8810
German-American. Sauerbraten, Hungarian goulash, wiener
schnitzel, wursts. Old oak tables and benches, rustic Bavarian atmosphere. Nightly music and barber shop quartet.

Oscar's Delmonico   56 Beaver St., BO 9-1180
Italian-Continental. Canelloni a la Oscar, Calf's liver Veneziana,
mushrooms trifolati, filet mignon stroganoff, lobster Newberg.
Dinner from $3.50. A la carte lunch from $2.50. Closed Sun.
Open Sat. for lunch only.

P

Pen & Pencil   205 East 45th St., MU 2-8660, MU 2-9825
American-Steak house. Charcoal broiled steaks, lobster, chops.
Favorite spot of newspapermen, account executives and stage stars.
A la carte lunch from $2.55; dinner from $3.75. Closed for lunch
Sat. & Sun.

Penthouse Club   30 Park Ave. So., PL 9-3561
Continental-American. Coq au vin, breast of cornish hen a la
Kiev, filet mignon. On a clear day, a superb view of Manhattan.
Lunch from $3.00; dinner from $5.00. Closed Sun. & holidays.

Per Bacco   140 East 27th St., LE 2-8699
French-Italian. Salt 'n Bocca per bacco. Garden dining area in
summer. Lunch from $2.25; dinner from $3.95. Closed Sun.

Philippine Garden   455 Second Ave., MU 6-1326
Philippine only. Stuffed shrimp, stuffed boneless chicken (*relye-
nong manok*). Good food and unpretentious decor matched by
even less unpretentious prices. Lunch from $1.00; dinner from
$2.50. Seven course lunch, $1.35. A la carte lunch from $1.00,
dinner from $1.50.

P. J. Moriarty's 213 West 33rd St., LO 3-3453
1034 Third Ave., TE 8-2438; 50 East 54th St., MU 8-6060
American-Irish. Prime ribs of beef, sliced beef steak, corned beef & cabbage, beef goulash, Irish lamb stew, steaks, chops, seafood, Irish coffee. A la carte lunch from $2.65; dinner from $3.50. All closed Sun. except Third Ave. Moriarty's.

Polonaise 230 East 51st St., PL 5-1961
Polish-continental. Cutlet de Polonaise, roast Long Island duckling bigarade. Lunch from $2.25; dinner a la carte from $3.25. Violin and piano music nightly. Closed Sun.

Q

Quo Vadis 26 East 63rd St., TE 8-0590
French. Lobster aux aromates, carrée d'agneau, persille moscatte, soufflé praline aux noisettes. A la carte lunch from $2.75; dinner from $4.50. Open Sun. for dinner only. Closed Sat. & Sun. during July & August.

R

Ruby Foo's 240 West 52nd St., CO 5-0705, PL 7-5965
Chinese. T'ang steak, barbecued baby spare ribs, boneless duck amandine, choo chin chow platter. Lunch from $1.25. A la carte dinner from $1.85. Open Sun. after 1 p.m.

Russian Tea Room 150 West 57th St., CO 5-0947
Russian. Not a tea room. Vodka, caviar, shaslik, beef stroganoff, borscht. Lunch from $2.25; dinner from $4.50.

S

Sardi's East 123 East 54th St., PL 1-6655
American-continental. Hot shrimp Sardi, Long Island duckling flambé, roast prime ribs of beef. Sardi double decker bus to whisk diners to the theater on time. Favorite with TV celebrities. A la carte lunch from $2.00; dinner from $2.50. Open Sat., Sun. & holidays for cocktails and dinner only.

Sardi's West 234 West 44th St., LA 4-0707
American-continental. Supreme of chicken Sardi, cannelloni au gratin, crabmeat Sardi. The original Sardi's, the after theater supper spot popular with stage people. A la carte only: lunch from $2.00; dinner from $2.50. Closed Sun.

Sea Fare, Sea Fare of the Aegean 44 West 8th St., AL 4-5646
1033 First Ave., PL 9-4176; 25 West 56th St., LT 1-0540
Seafood. Mussels mariniere, oysters Rockefeller. Lunch from $1.85. A la carte lunch & dinner from $1.95. Service bar only.

Seventeen Barrow 17 Barrow St., CH 2-9726
Continental. Beef stroganoff, Caucasian shashlyk, coq au vin, duck à l'orange. Two fire places, candlelight, old village atmos-

phere, music. Dinner from $2.00. Open for dinner only. Wine & beer but no liquor.

Shavey Lee's Tung Sai   32 Mulberry St., BE 3-7747
Chinese-Cantonese. Lunch from $1.00. Complete dinner $4.40. Closed Mon.

Sieburg's Buffet 45 Nassau St., BA 7-6149; 29 New St., DI 4-2892
German-American. Beef ála mode, sauerbraten, corn beef & cabbage, beef stew, buffet style. Entrees start at 45c. Open for breakfast and lunch only. Closed Sat. & Sun.

Stanley Chin's Tai Yat Low   22 Mott St., WO 2-3892
Chinese-Cantonese. Gai kew wor bar, mo goo, rainbow lobster, crabmeat soong. Lunch from $1.10. A la carte dinner from $1.45. Family dinner from $2.75. Seven course dinner, $4.00. No bar.

Stark's   Madison Ave. at 78th St., LE 5-5377
     Broadway at 90th St., TR 3-6462
American. Roast beef, baked virginia ham, eggs anyway, home made pastries. Lunch à la carte from $1.60, dinner from about $2.20. Service bar at Madison Ave.; no bar at Broadway.

Steinberg's Dairy Restaurant   Broadway & 82nd St., EN 2-2030
Jewish-European. Gefuelte fish, blintzes, kreplach, pirogen, borscht, potato pancakes, smoked fish. Lunch from $1.50. A la carte dinner from $1.45. Open for breakfast. No bar.

Steuben House   20 East 22nd St., GR 7-9346
German-continental. Weiner schnitzer, paprika schnitzel. Restaurant & rathskeller. A la carte lunch from $1.75; dinner from $1.95. Closed Sat., Sun. & holidays.

Steuben Tavern   163 West 47th St., JU 6-2682
Bavarian-American. Wild game in season, sauerbraten, schnitzels. Lunch from 99c, dinner from $2.75. A la carte lunch from 95c, dinner from $1.75.

Swiss Pavilion   38 East 50th St., EL 5-8680
Swiss. Fondue bourguignone, cheese fondue. Lunch from $2.75; dinner from $4.75. Closed Sun.

T

Tavern-on-the-Green   Central Park W. at 67th St., TR 3-3200
Continental. Prime ribs, steaks, lobsters. French, Swiss, German specialties. Outdoor garden dining. Nightly orchestra and dancing. Lunch from $2.00; dinner from $3.50. A la carte lunch from $1.75; dinner from $3.50.

Teddy's   219 West Broadway, WO 6-2180
French-Italian. Lobster Newburg, scampi, antipasto. Lunch from $1.50; dinner from $6.50. A la carte lunch from $1.50. Closed Sun.

Teheran   44 West 44th St., MU 2-6588
Italian-Persian-American. Shish kebab, tchillow, chicken Soraya,

lobster fra diavolo, canelloni, steaks and chops. Lunch from $2.00; dinner from $3.75. A la carte lunch from $1.75; dinner from $2.00. Closed Sunday. Closed Sat. for lunch.

Toffenetti   1482 Broadway, LA 4-4523
American. Ham & sweets, American smorgäsbord. Lunch from $1.59; dinner from $3.75 (all you can eat). Regular lunch from $.75, dinner from $2.30. A la carte from $1.10. Background music.

Toots Shor   33 West 52nd St., JU 2-6000
American. Roast beef, chicken pot pie, Yankee pot roast, potato pancakes, London broil. Everything a la carte. Lunch from $2.50, dinner from $3.25. Supper from 10 a.m. to 2 a.m.

Top of the Six's   666 Fifth Ave., PL 7-6662
French-American. Flaming desserts. Superb view of New York from the top of the 39-story Tishman building. Lunch from $2.35; dinner from $5.45. A la carte lunch from $2.35; dinner from $5.50.

Trader Vic's   58th St. & Fifth Ave., EL 5-2600
Polynesian-continental. Indonesian lamb roast, Javanese sates, crab Rangoon, barbecued meats, fish, poultry. A la carte lunch from $3.10; dinner from $4.00.

√ **Twenty-One Club**   21 West 52nd St., JU 2-7200
French-American. Malayan hen, venison, English sole, terrapin, Malpeque oysters. Main Specialty: the great number of celebrities from all fields that come to dine and be seen. A la carte from $4.50.

V

Vesuvio   163 West 48th St., CI 5-6138
Italian. Veal rollatini fiet signon in Marsala wine, beef braciola ragu, lasanga, manicotti, baked seafood Vesuvio. Lunch from $2.75; dinner from $4.75. A la carte lunch from $1.50; dinner from $2.00.

W

√ **Whyte's**   145 Fulton St., CO 7-2233; 344 West 57th St., JU 6-7900
American. Seafood, curries, steaks, chops, home made bread & pastries. Lower Manhattan dining landmark for more than a half a century. Dinner from $3.00. A la carte lunch from $2. Closed Sun.

X

Xochitl   146 West 46th St., PL 7-1325
Mexican. Tacos, enchiladas, tamales, tostadas, quacamole, chile con carne, tortillas, Mexican beer. Lunch from $2.50; dinner from $3.50. A la carte lunch & dinner from $1.50.

Y

Ye Old Chop House   101 Cedar St., RE 2-6166
American. English mutton chops, game and seafood in season. A la carte lunch & dinner from $3.25. Closed Sat. & Sun.

Nightclubs

Alameda Room   118 West 57th St., CO 5-0535
Latin American revue and dancing. Min. Closed Mon.

Basin Street East   137 East 48th St., PL 2-4444
Big names in jazz. Cover charge. Closed Sun.

Birdland   1687 Broadway, JU 6-7333
Straight jazz from start to finish. Admission charge, Minimum.

Blue Angel   152 East 55th St., PL 3-5998
Top drawer star attractions. Admission charge.

Bon Soir   40 West 8th St., OR 4-0531
Variety entertainment. Minimum. Closed Mon.

Chateau Madrid   42 West 58th St., PL 3-3773
Star Latin American entertainment and dancing. Minimum.

Copacabana   10 East 60th St., PL 8-0900
Big, plushy club with large (and luscious) chorus line and big name talent. Dancing. Minimum.

El Chico   80 Grove St., CH 2-4645
Reasonably small, intimate night club featuring Spanish entertainment, good food and dancing. Minimum. Closed Sun.

El Morocco   307 East 54th St., PL 2-5079
Café society's pet club — one of New York's most expensive. Dancing. Cover charge.

Embers   161 East 54th St., PL 9-3228
A New York jazz spot with steaks and chops another feature attraction. Minimum after 9:30 p.m.

Empire Room   Park Avenue & 49th St., EL 5-3000
Waldof Astoria's plush club featuring big name talent and dancing. Cover charge. Closed Sun.

Hawaiian Room   Lexington Avenue & 48th St., PL 5-4400
Hawaiian entertainment and food in the Hotel Lexington. Dancing. Cover charge. Closed Sun.

International Theater-Restaurant
    B'way & 52nd St., CI 7-3070
Lavish floor show twice nightly. Dancing. Minimum.

Latin Quarter   200 West 48th St., CI 6-1735
Over-sized plushy nightclub specializing in the abbreviated costumes of its long-stemmed chorus line. Dancing. Minimum.

La Zambra   14 East 60th St., EL 5-4774
Combines excellent Spanish cuisine with equally excellent flamenco guitars and entertainment. Closed Sun.

Liborio (see restaurants)

Metropole   Seventh Avenue at 48th St., CI 5-0088
A New York jazz "institution" since the 1920's and 30's with performances atop the bar. Cover charge.

Nick's   170 West 10th St., CH 2-6683
Dixieland has been reigning supreme in this Village landmark since it first took over New York.

Peppermint Lounge   128 West 45th St., CI 5-9363
Chief claim to fame: gave birth to the twist. Floor show and dancing. Cover charge.

Persian Room, Plaza 9   Fifth Avenue & 59th St., PL 9-3000
Plaza Hotel's intimate clubs. The first features stellar entertainment and cover charge; the second, Julius Monk's satirical revues and minimum. Closed Sun.

Roundtable   151 East 50th St., PL 8-0310
Presently specializing in belly dancing, thugh has been known to feature jazz. Cover charge except Sun.

Stork Club   3 East 53rd St., PL 3-1940
A café society favorite and expensive. Dancing. Cover charge after 9 p.m.

Second City at Square East   15 West 4th St., AL 4-0480
The Second City troupe puts on some wonderful satirical sketches in this Village spot. Only snacks available.

Upstairs at the Downstairs   37 West 56th St., JU 2-1244
Sophisticated entertainment. Minimum. Closed Sun.

Viennese Lantern   242 East 79th St., TR 9-7760
Features continental shows with Viennese food. Closed Mon.

Village Barn   52 West 8th St., GR 3-8841
Variety show with square dancing and country games. Minimum.

Useful Telephone Numbers

New York City Department of Parks	RE 4-1000
New York Convention and Visitors Bureau	MU 7-1300
New York Daily News Information Bureau	MU 2-1234
New York Public Library	OX 5-4200
New York Times Information	LA 4-1000
Travelers Aid Society	OR 9-0200
Weather Reports	WE 6-1212